The
S. JACQUES COHEN
STORY

A WWII HOLOCAUST
Survivor from Amsterdam

S. JACQUES COHEN
AND DR. E.J. NIKKEL

The S. Jacques Cohen Story - A WWII Survivor From Amsterdam

ISBN: 978-1505327243

First Edition, 2014

Table of Contents

PROLOGUE

This book is dedicated to Kuintje Griffioen Cohen, my beloved mother, who, during those terrible times of the War, hid my family and dedicated her life to helping other Jews stay alive with food and clothing. I love her dearly for her heroism.

Kuintje Griffioen Cohen (my beloved mother; pictured left) and me, Samuel Jacques Cohen, with my loveable pugs.

My name is Samuel Jacques Cohen, youngest son of Levie and Kuintje Cohen. I was born in Ostende, Belgium, on 13 December 1926. My parents came from Holland and were owners of a hotel with a large bar and dining room in the city. In those years, people would come from England to the horse races in Ostende and it was common for the owners of establishments to serve important customers themselves. Shortly before I was born, my father was opening a large beer barrel and got a long metal splinter in his hand. The doctor who came out was sleepy and accidently cut the tendon in my father's finger. His mistake caused my father's hand to become deformed. At the time that I was born, it was a long standing Jewish tradition that a male baby would be circumcised. Because of my father's injury, everything took longer and he and my mother never got around to having me circumcised. I mention this now as later in the book you will discover how this oversight was one of many factors that helped keep me alive through WWII.

Eventually, my Father's injury was so bad that he could no longer serve his customers and had to sell the establishment. Our family moved back to Amsterdam in 1929.

The reason I'm writing about my experiences during World War II is that whenever the War comes up in conversation, people ask me about my childhood during the War. When I tell them something about this period, they all say that I should write down my experiences for future reference so that people should never forget how terrible those times were and how it impacted so many lives. This book is my contribution the betterment of mankind and to make sure that my story does not go forgotten.

As my story begins, I'll start with my understanding of the history of the Holocaust and WWII. Hitler had provided assurances to Holland that we would not be attacked, however history demonstrated that this was one of many of the lies he told. The Holocaust was so complicated, confusing and overwhelming that many survivors feel the need to speak out about the atrocities, brutality and horror of it. For me, I know this to be quite self-evident. It goes without saying that each country, ethnic group and individual experienced the events surrounding the Holocaust differently, yet with many elements in common. This is my story and how it impacted my life and impacts me to this day. My story is that of a boy turning into a man in Holland, witnessing horrors no one should ever see or experience and still dealing with the repercussions almost seventy years later.

After the War, the Diary of Anne Frank became the most widely read book about this time in Holland's history. It detailed her hiding in the attic during this World War. Anne was not the only child and her family was not the only family that experienced the inhumanity of this War. There were thousands of other Jewish families and children in Holland who lived through horrors, constant fear, and the inhumane atrocities of this War.

Anne's story helped the world understand what it was like to live and die in Hitler's Holocaust. For many of us who lived through the War years cannot handle reading, seeing a play or watching a movie based on any accounts of this time in history. It hits too close to our own lives and experiences and brings back all the memories as if we are living it all over again and again. Today, we call this Post-Traumatic Stress Disorder (P.T.S.D.). Whatever the medical term is, these triggers are too close to what we suffered and experienced when it resurfaces. Other times, the P.T.S.D. brings up long-suppressed memories and emotions. While we do want others to know that there were many of us who suffered, and sometimes living was much harder than just having our lives being over.

In 1939, I was 12 years old and I was 18 years old in 1945 when Germany and Japan surrendered. It was the end of the War, but not remotely the end of its destructive forces on people's lives everywhere.

In my life, there were six pivotal years from 1939 through 1946, that I use as chapter breaks. The War that was to end all wars defined my life, my family's life and much of the world's life. I've added in some historical context to these years and my memories to provide context for your understanding.

This is my fake ID without the "J" for Jood. Jood is Dutch for Jew. I used my fake ID when I went underground to save my life.

Chapter One: 1939

My brother, Leo and I would visit our grandparents regularly in Zandvoort. I was 12 years old and Leo was 16 years old. My grandfather's name was Salomon Cohen and my grandmother's name was Leentje van der Bijl Cohen. We lovingly referred to them as Opa (grandfather) and Oma (grandmother).

Opa always enjoyed and anticipated our visits when we biked the 25 miles from Amsterdam to visit them at Zandvoort. We could smell the freshly-baked cookies upon our arrival. We thoroughly enjoyed Opa's cookies more than Oma's as hers were not as fresh.

On every visit, my brother Leo entertained us with musical compositions performed on the beautiful grand piano. Opa and Oma would clap and reminisce about the old days. We happily listened to their stories, even when they disagreed on the details. Their stories gave us insight and pride into our Cohen family heritage.

The town in which my grandparents lived in was a luxurious beach town full of travellers, tourists and locals. My brother and I would spend hours in the water rough-housing, swimming and playing. At this time of my life everything was fresh, full of hope and promise. It was also a great time of just plain fun! We enjoyed playing in the water, wrestling each other as we had done for all of our lives. We cherished our time at the beach with our grandparents, especially our Opa. Oma was wonderful, however she was not as playful and quick to smile as Opa. Opa watched my brother and I from his vantage point from his blanket on the dunes. From the water, we could see him smile and the sparkle of love in his eyes.

The next day was Saturday, the Sabbath or *Shabbat*, the day of joy and rest, so tonight, Oma lit the Shabbat candles and Opa recited the blessings for wine and bread. Opa, being an Orthodox

TOP: Picture of my grandfather, great-grandfather and various great-aunts and other relatives.

BOTTOM: Picture taken on 8 May 1940 in Zandvoort, two days before the War in front of their home and store.

Jew, followed the steps of donning his *Tallit* (prayer shawl) and laying *Tefillin* (a small box with prayers inside with some ties) on it. It is tied around the forehead with the little box in front and straps around one arm and is used only by Orthodox Jews for prayer at morning services on weekdays. Opa prayed and recited beautiful words that stirred within. We boys enjoyed listening to Opa's rhythmic chants carefully enunciating those special, sacred words. Besides, Oma's delicious meal would make waiting worthwhile: potatoes, white fish, fresh vegetables and homemade bread. Leo and I found it very comical that Opa and Oma each had their separate butter dish and would always do some bickering about this or that. Opa would slather his butter on his and our bread, but Oma was stingy and would mumble about wasting good butter and what was so wrong about being a little careful and saving. Opa's eyes would twinkle as he teased Oma and he gave us boys a look that told us that he loved this special woman. We were again reminded of the safety and comfort of our family bonds, something that served us well in the horrible years coming swooping down on us from the northeast. Unfortunately, nothing could keep Leo safe enough in those following years.

Later, with a cup of coffee (mine had lots of milk in it) and an almond pastry, the family sat in the front room and listened to Leo's mesmerizing, memorized masterpieces on the grand piano. He was one of the best classical pianists in Holland. Listening to him breathe life into those notes was pure pleasure, even for me, a rambunctious 12 year old boy. I idolized my big brother. I admired him even as I, like many younger siblings, made sure I wasn't just like him. Constant comparisons drove me farther away from wanting to be a "good boy like Leo" and forge my own pathways like my great-great-Opa Cohen who had come from Spain when the Jewish persecution became too much for his family. I had no clue or understanding about persecution,

Many people daily wore provincial garb. This is in the village of Volendam which was not very far from Zandvoort (from "Portraits of War: A Canadian in Holland During WWII, Photographic Journal of Captain William J. Klyn, 1945"). Dutch in provincial garb (Photograph in Public Domain).

let alone persecution just because a person was a Jew. I could almost feel his drive in my frame, encouraging me to be a man he would be proud of. I would soon need that strength desperately.

Leo and I loved it when Opa would tell stories about our family or Holland or even go back as far as our family in Spain. It made us feel bonded with our forefathers. As we sat around in the front room, Opa cleared his throat and then started, "Speaking of Amsterdam...," and he shared more history, more memories and more dreams for the future. The four of us settled into our family history that was intertwined with the history of this land of ours, watching the character of our family built up just as the land we walked on was built up and taken back from the sea.

Our grandparents' specialty store of custom-made baby clothes and other baby things was connected to their house. We went into that part of their home and spent hours cleaning, dusting, and tidying up, moving boxes and helping out at their store, Le Petit Papillon, *The Little Butterfly*. It was well worth it and neither of us minded spending more time with Opa and Oma. I loved watching them interact with customers. They were so friendly, helpful and kind.

Our grandparents had once lived in Amsterdam where they owned a large department store downtown. They became "extremely wealthy" according to my father. They owned a very nicely decorated three-story home and had many of the amenities that money could buy. Only really wealthy people owned their own homes. Most people in Amsterdam lived in apartments.

Sometimes our father, Levie, would tell my brother and I about the jewelry and wonderful clocks Opa loved to collect. After Opa and Oma sold the department store, they kept the four-story building. Later, they lost the building to the Nazis who confiscated it and many other Jews' buildings and properties. They retired to the beach village of Zandvoort to a very comfortable house. Just to keep themselves active, they opened up a specialty store offering handmade baby clothing and accessories.

Parents and grandparents from all over the Netherlands, Belgium, Luxembourg and even countries farther away would come to the beach and buy the shawls, blankets, transporters and other specialties. Opa and Oma had a well-deserved reputation for carrying unusual and beautiful products and for being fair on prices. Plus, they were wonderful shopkeepers with lots of stories, always making their customers feel welcome and special.

Opa made efforts to make Leo and me feel good about whatever we did, boosting our confidence and teaching us both to be self-sufficient. Opa was a very giving man and always snuck us some money to buy something, especially candies. He understood the hearts of his grandsons and how important it was to have some money and "be a man." This had a large impact on the way I look at money. I liked feeling like a young man instead of a boy.

While we there, Leo and I showed off our strength and our grandparents rewarded us with a few well placed oohs and aahs to encourage us. Although Leo was four years older than me, I was the rough and tumble one while my only sibling was the complacent and obedient one. At home, all I ever heard was, "Why can't you be more like your older brother?" Opa seemed to understand and would encourage me to stay strong and told me I could make it through anything – just use my *koph* (mind).

I was more than ready for 6th grade and all the rest of life. At least that's what I thought, there at the beach when I was 12.

What I did not realize was this was to be the last long visit we had at the seashore with my grandparents in Zandvoort. I couldn't dwell on these memories for very long or the sadness of the simplicity of life lost would overwhelm me.

I look back fondly at these memories of a young Jewish boy that had a seemingly carefree life. I was free, innocent and could hardly wait for my future to begin. If I saw him now, I would no longer recognize him as me.

Me being Jewish was never an issue. I was growing up in a beautiful country, with a wonderful family and living a good life.

With autumn just around the corner, school would be starting soon and it would be more difficult to break away and make the 25 mile trip. Leo and I both knew it, too, and linger, in no hurry to leave our grandparents and go back to the constraints of school and weekends working at our father's factory. But all good things must end; Leo had to get back for his lessons at the

Bach Conservatory in Amsterdam and I was entering 6th grade. Very soon, too soon, summer turned to fall. Where our lives transformed from idyllic to horrific. Much of my understanding of the war at this time was based on what my Opa had told me. Hitler's push to have the supreme race of Aryans rule the world meant the annihilation of all Jews. Opa told us of how Hitler's German *Blitzkrieg* invaded Poland during September 1939, immediately capturing over 3 million Jews, segregating them in walled off ghettos or holding areas where they were murdered, beaten, raped, died of disease and starvation. Notwithstanding, Hitler was not pleased that the death rate was not higher and that it was taking too long to exterminate the Jews to extinction. This prompted the mass execution of the Jews by the thousands, until the shooting was deemed too expensive, inefficient and demoralizing for the German soldiers.

The news of the 1938 annexation of Austria and the occupation of the Czech Sudetenland from Germany alarmed Opa to the point of anxiety. In fact, nearly all the news transmitted was a source for constant panic and terror for everyone that had cause to fear.

"Too little too late" defined us Dutch. The Netherlands hadn't been in a war for over a century and had only recently mobilized any of their forces. None of it was in time. On 3 September, Britain declared War on Germany. France joined Britain because both of these countries had promised to protect Poland. The Australians promised their support, too, and now, World War II was upon Europe, headed toward the rest of us and many knew it. Our country strongly declared our neutrality and hoped it would stick. In late 1939, Hitler's government issued their policy for us in the Netherlands: "The new Reich has endeavored to continue the traditional friendship with Holland. It has not taken over [sic] any existing differences

Hitler demanded his SS troops marry and bear children, so often there would be mass weddings, necessary to produce perfect Aryans. (Photograph in Public Domain).

A poster of the sought after perfect Aryan family.

between the two countries and has not created any new ones" – German Guarantee of Neutrality, 6 October 1939.

Many of the Dutch didn't believe their German Guarantee of Neutrality would be honored, but had hoped that they would. We had no idea what was ahead for us.

Britain was the Allied's Forces greatest strength at this time. Sir Winston Churchill, Prime Minister of Britain during WWII was an encouragement to all of us and we would listen to him speak on BBC Radio throughout the War. He would not give up the fight and he encouraged us.

As Hitler moved through Poland and possibly toward us, our Dutch government tried to obtain new arms for our ill-equipped forces. Most of the weapons purchased never arrived due to shortages and routes blockades. Now, the Nazis were pushing out their boundaries, again.

Hitler had been in power in Germany since January 1933. He and his Nazi party took over power in Germany with bold promises and propaganda. The goal was to build Germany a super race of tall blond people called "Aryans," the "best in the world."

In Hitler's mind, there was absolutely no room for Slavs, gypsies, blacks, the intelligentsia, homosexuals, dwarfs and, worst of all in Hitler's mind, Jews, whom he blamed for Germany's defeat in World War I. The rumor was that Hitler's father, Alois, was a bastard Jew, born of the rape of his mother, a servant in a Jewish home in Austria. If so, Hitler was part Jew and yet he despised his own people or maybe since his Oma had been raped, that is partly why he hated us. Whatever the reason, this was no simple hate.

To carry out his supreme dream of building Germany into a super race and power, all Jews in Germany had to be "gone," either by deportation or extermination. Hitler's slogan, "Deutschland uber alles" (Germany above everything), meant absolutely no Jews and the Nazis immediately implemented his anti-Jewish regime of terror and horror. Between his seizing power in 1933 until the end of the War, over six million Jews were killed. "Killed" is too soft a word for the horrific deaths most of these people experienced. As much as Hitler hated Jews, during this time he also brutally murdered over five million other people who he deemed not worthy to live. This included the physically and mentally disabled, Poles, Jehovah's Witnesses, any dissident and any communists, both Roma and Sinti. He easily added minorities to his list of disposable, sub-human people.

The method Hitler had used to control the German Jews was that he started immediately taking away all rights from them. We would soon understand his method because he used the same evil tactic in every country they conquered. Third Reich Nazis (short for National Socialist German Workers' Party) were

LEFT: Sir Winston Churchill, Prime Minister of the United Kingdom from 1940 to 1945 (battlefield-site.co.uk).
RIGHT: Dogfight in sky above Big Ben in London (Photograph in Public Domain).

14

Polish Jews being herded to concentration camps in 1939 after the uprising in the Warsaw ghetto. Anti-Semitic propaganda in Germany

(United States Holocaust Memorial Museum).

poised to strike over and over again in each country using the same tactics.

When Jews had heard about their brothers and sisters being attacked on the 9th and 10th of November 1938 by Nazi unrestrained anti-Semitic violence in an event infamously known as *"Kristallnacht," Crystal Night* or *the Night of Shattered Glass.* Broken windows and glass shards covered the streets throughout Germany. The Brown Shirt Nazi storm troopers went through the streets shouting profanities and, "Where are the Jews?" They hauled off as many of the Jewish men they could find, made them walk through the streets so the Germans could spit on them as they sent them to prison and concentration camps.

The Nazis broke down the doors and smashed all the windows of Jewish shops and synagogues. They beat and killed many Jews, threw them from windows to their deaths, looted their apartments, burned or desecrated synagogues. They also took prayer books and The Torah, stomped and threw them on manure piles or lit them on fire. Personal property of the Jews was destroyed. The level of hatred and violence against the Jews had increased exponentially over these two abominable days.

We in Holland should have paid more attention to this event, the annexation of Austria and then the invasion of Poland. We should have prepared ourselves, but we didn't comprehend the depth of Hitler's evil plans. We were in denial that any such thing could happen in our safe, neutral little country.

The Nazis spent the next years sending thousands of German and Polish Jews to concentration camps, where most of them died during what became known as "The Holocaust". The Jews were burned or gassed in crematoriums and then dumped into mass graves.

Jews that made it out alive, were but mere shadows of their former selves. Their faces gaunt, heads-sheared, their spirits broken, hollow-eyed and deeply emaciated bodies, never to be the same again.

The Germans had not yet defined what their *Final Solution* was for the Jews. Later it became clear that it was the complete annihilation of all Jews.

TOP: German Jews were rounded up and marched to prisons.
BOTTOM: Rollcall at Buchenwald concentration camp shortly after
Kristallnacht
(Source: United States Holocaust Memorial Museum).

The "Holocaust" referred to the years in the 1930's and 1940's of the Nazis' "final solution" of destroying the Jews, elderly, ill or other ethnic or cultural groups Hitler deemed unworthy of existence. Many German Jews had realized earlier that they had no future in this hostile Germany and had tried to leave for safer countries. No countries, worldwide, were willing to let the German refugees in, including the United States. One of the only countries which had accepted them was the Netherlands. Holland had accepted 35,000 German Jews, including Otto Frank who brought his daughters, Anne and Margot, and his wife to our country. But even Holland quit taking in Jewish refugees in 1938 because they were overrunning us and we were still dealing with the depression. By this time in 1939, the German Jews had nowhere to run except Singapore, Shanghai and Argentina where many went.

In World War I, the Netherlands (a small country about the size of Maryland), was neutral as it bordered both Germany and Belgium. Hitler had again assured Holland it would not be attacked. As German Jews had flooded into Holland, hanging onto their naïve belief in Hitler's word, all Jews in this neutral country would soon find out how wrong they were to believe that they would be left alone.

At the end of this year, I turned 13 and my life was never the same. We had a celebration and I felt more mature, but the next few years matured me beyond my years. I witnessed many atrocities, saw the devastation caused by brutality and lived through five of the most evil years in the history of the world.

Chapter Two: 1940

Although there was a lot of grown-up talk going on, I caught bits and pieces of conversations, sensing the unrest and concern, but not knowing the full implications. The adults

Kristallnacht, the Night of Broken Glass. Destroyed stained glass from Zerrennerstrasse synagogue and Jewish shops' glass windows shattered (United States Holocaust Memorial Museum).

*Boerneplatz synagogue in flames and, afterwards, with only one wall standing
(United States Holocaust Memorial Museum).*

talked a lot, almost in secrecy. I wanted to hear everything. So, I would pretend I wasn't listening, but I heard more than my family thought I had heard. Some of the snippets talked about how Poland had been overrun by the Germans. Britain and France declared war against Germany. Would the United States join the Allies? Would the Germans attack Belgium next? German Jews had moved in with the Vermeers down the street. The Boumas had sold their house and left for Dutch Aruba even though they were Gentiles (not Jewish). The Reformed Van Wyhes, Nikkels and Van Maanens moved to Iowa in the United States. Soon they wrote back that they were allowed to buy land and they didn't have to pay to go to church. Many of their relatives tried to leave and join them for this freedom and because of the unrest here. More names, more people moving away, so many more things that I couldn't remember it all. There was the discussion of where the Polish Jews, German Jews and other Jews would be relocated to, but no one was sure where.

I was now in 6th grade. I liked school, not so much for the learning, although that was pretty interesting, too, but for the social time. I had some good friends whom I had seen only spo-radically during the summer. Now we had more time together. Henrik was probably one of my best friends just because of his quick mind and risk taking. Together we would explore *"Groot Mokum"* (Jewish slang for Amsterdam) after school. We found new pathways, over and around the canals, to our homes and other neighborhoods, exploring out to the flats of the suburbs. We loved the bells of hundreds of bicycles and added ours to the melee, as the car horns and noise of streetcars clashed. We loved the life in our city of Amsterdam.

We had so much fun when I was growing up, before the War. There were always lots of other kids to play with, tear around with and grab life with! We had bicycle races, went sledding and then went skating on the canals when they were frozen hard. Amsterdam, like all of Holland, was immaculately cared for and kept up. The Dutch are known for their cleanliness and the streets were scrubbed and everything kept clean and neat. This cleanliness included keeping ourselves clean. Since no houses or apartments were equipped with showers, once a week my mother would give me a coin and I would go to the bathhouse and get cleaned up just like every other person in Amsterdam. Later, during the War, I longed to clean up in that old bath house again. Things were wonderful and I thought this was the way my world would always be and that I would always be this carefree, happy and safe. Even I knew there were dark, foreboding clouds along the edges now. Yes, the transformation had begun and would soon accelerate.

My friends and I knew the streets, alleys, backyards and canals very well because it was still safe to wander around and explore. We would sit and look at the reflections of the houses and their gabled facades in the black waters of the canals. We always brought bread crumbs for the ducks and geese. Amsterdam was named after the river Amstel where it met the North Sea. We were a natural harbor for all sorts of shipping from all different countries. Often, I would watch the ships coming into port and fantasize about going off to faraway countries, living a life of adventure, bravado and honor. I would make my family proud! I had talked to people in the United States and other places in Europe who would sit along highways when they were kids and name the different state license plates on vehicles going by. In Amsterdam, we would name the different country flags on the big ships passing through.

Leo and I went to the public school for general education. Let me explain a little more of our culture so you will understand how our history had greased the wheels for the German machine to take us over. All religious instruction had ended in public schools almost a century ago, but Catholics had their own schools as did a few Protestants/Calvinists. The religious differences affected the social and political life of our country. History class taught us that our society had religiously segregated into organized groups (Protestant, Catholic and secular) which, to a large extent, eliminated most internal conflict. The third group, the secular group, had split into the working class/socialist group and the pro-business/liberal group. Each of the four groups had their own social entities, including churches (except for the secular), schools, labor unions or guilds, youth clubs and even newspapers. Each group had its own radio station, so listening to the news of the day was profoundly affected by which group's radio you heard. If you were a member of one group, you very rarely had anything to do with the other three groups, including business dealings or even marrying someone from different religious backgrounds. The Jewish community was an even smaller group within the major group. For us Jews, people from other groups were Gentiles, which just meant they weren't Jewish.

This "pluralism" in our country worked because of the cooperation of the civic leaders, but this cooperation would fall apart during WWII. Smooth running politics and public life would end in catastrophe. The originators of the concept of everyone being a part of only one group had no understanding of how this would play into the hands of the Nazis. It would soon be very easy to cut out, ostracize and relocate a group of "non-desirables." People of the Netherlands were quite proud of their tolerance of religious beliefs and proud that religious persecution had totally ceased over a quarter of a century ago in this progressive country. Yet, how quickly that persecution would return with horrific wickedness, smothering decades of so-called "growth"!

Opa called often from Zandvoort, wanting to talk to his son, Levie, because he was very concerned with Germany's plans.

Our country had just gone through our Great Depression and economic stability was nowhere near restored. There was still high unemployment and widespread poverty. A war could throw all of our efforts to the wind. *"Jah*, we had the large public works project that built the *Afsluitdijk*, damming off the Zuider Zee and creating the Ijsselmeer Lake, cutting Amsterdam off from being open to the North Sea for the first time ever. World War II will go way beyond that in scope and we aren't ready; the military just wasn't prepared," Opa would go on as Father patiently listened.

"We don't stand a chance if Hitler comes to Holland," Opa would complain to my father. "Even now, our government has been ordering new weapons, but the munitions plants have run out of everything because all of Europe is trying to get their hands on armaments. Too much unrest in the country already." Quietly, Father would reassure him, calming him down by talking about Opa's friend who had worked on the Big Project. "Ach, too many good men have died even though the country needed the work. America was doing the same thing with their Hoover Dam, trying to work themselves out of the Depression," Opa worried, but soon, Father would have him calmed down and even laughing. He was a master on the telephone. Opa only called when Oma was out doing some errands. He didn't want to unnecessarily worry her, though she knew this man well enough to know what he was going through and she was grateful for her son, my father, who would calm her dear husband down, for a time anyway.

Father wasn't outwardly worried, although he couldn't help but know more than he wanted to since his father was keeping up so well on what was going on across Europe. Father had traveled to Germany often for business and had an insight into what was going on there. We were neutral and Hitler had promised he would not attack us. Father told us he was sure Hitler would honor his word and besides, Opa was an old man and worried too much – at least that's what he would say when we were around.

Father reasoned with us one evening that our country controlled the mouths of the Schelde, the Rhine and the Meuse Rivers. Germany wouldn't bother us because they wouldn't want to disrupt their industrial areas of the Ruhr and they needed to ship their products from the Dutch port of Rotterdam, the largest port in all of Europe. Besides, Father said, if Germany invaded us, Britain and/or France would counterattack as they defended their own interests on our various rivers. Father had reasoned it out and it was settled in his mind. We soon found out that logic and reason did not play a large part in this War and that Hitler's ideology would have massive consequences.

My father had been an importer of materials and often went to Germany on business. He knew good and well what was

Amsterdam postcard (Photograph in Public Domain).

*We always had fun along the over 100 canals no matter the season
(Photograph in Public Domain) and enjoyed skating along the frozen
canals in winter (Beeldbank WO2).*

*Child with pillow learning to skate (Photograph in Public Domain) and
boys like us having bicycle races (National Monument of Amersfoort).*

going on over there and it worried him, too. Actually, Father
now owned his own manufacturing business of household
articles and still did some traveling to Germany. My mother was
the secretary and that is how they met. He had experienced

much of what Germany was facing and he, too, could see what was coming. He had made many friends in Germany and he was worried about them, too. If war came, it would not fare well for us or for any Jews.

As the months of talk and speculation sped by, Leo and I were looking forward to summer holiday, already planning our first bicycle ride to Zandvoort. Ah, just to smell the ocean again and to be back in the small beach town in the summer with Opa and Oma on the lovely, wide dark yellow beach! But that was not to be ever again.

On 10 May 1940, a day forever ingrained in our memories, the Germans invaded Holland, Belgium and Luxemburg. Our whole family was still sleeping when the air raid sirens started to wail in the middle of the night and went on and on for a long time. We all woke up in a panic and quickly ran outside where everyone in the neighborhood congregated in stark terror, arms wrapped around themselves for some little comfort. Many stood by in shocked silence while others screamed hysterically. We saw the German planes overhead and several shouted that they saw paratroopers coming down from the sky. There were battalions of them dropping into our country, our city and our lives.

We were shocked by the loud explosions and heard the shooting. That was the first time I had ever heard such sounds. Soon, I would become all too familiar to that awful sound. We knew we were at War and were being invaded. My Father was a volunteer air-raid warden and had been moving through the crowd, calming them as much as he could possibly do through words of encouragement and hope. He had returned back to where our family was standing as we looked up in to the sky. I can still hear the prophetic words of my father, "This is going to be the end of all Jews in Holland." How true his words turned out to be.

Our army was not a formidable force and things had not

improved since our Great Depression. Our ill-placed hope in The League of Nations and their politicians proved to be ineffective. Our compulsory military service that had once been two years was reduced to six months years earlier. The young men would return from their compulsory service and joke that they were in training barely long enough to learn which end of the gun should be aimed at the enemy. The chuckling was over now. Our military was very small, unprepared and lacked the armaments they needed to protect us.

We had approximately 20 battalions, Those battalions were not ready for battle let alone war with Germany. Most of our soldiers carried carbines (muskets) from the 19th century. Our air force, *Luchtvaartafdeeling*, had only a few modern aircraft and could not take on the German *Luftwaffe* (air force). The *Luftwaffe* freely roamed our skies and the German ground troops were there to seize our bridges and airfields and that's what they were doing with very little resistance.

The Netherlands had not fought a major military campaign since the 1760's, and the strength of its armed forces had gradually dwindled. The Dutch decided not to ally themselves with anyone, and kept out of all European wars especially World War I. Our military was not prepared, trained, or ready when Germany's invaded us. Not one of our commanders had anticipated the invasion to come from paratroopers landing behind our lines all across our land. Our commanders were instead watching for tanks at our borders. To say they were ill prepared for the invasion is an understatement.

Germany thought they would overrun us rather quickly because they had researched the areas of attack. In fact, the watchtower near the Grebbe Line was not even closed because our Prime Minister, Dirk Jan de Geer, said it "would harm the Dutch economy." Well then, his foolishness surely did harm our economy now, didn't it?! The espionage was completed and the Germans knew exactly where our bunkers were and how to make them useless to us. Later in the War, Dirk thought Germany was going to win and he tried to negotiate with Hitler. Queen Wilhelmina was instrumental in kicking him out of his position as Prime Minister and we were grateful to her for that. She was smart and a tough, courageous Queen.

Contrary to the Nazi thinking, our Dutch soldiers fought back with more strength than expected. Paratroopers were even kept out of The Hague itself. The Germans had planned that we (Belgium, Luxembourg and us) would be a one or two day conquest in their march toward France. True, much of our country was quickly overrun, but the northern attack was stopped in its tracks. The attack near Grebbeberg was halted.

In the south, the battles were like a see-saw, but one bridge over the Maas River at Rotterdam was still held by us although the Germans were trying hard to capture it. Their plan was to take the 9th Panzer Division across into Rotterdam. Some of the German divisions were trying to land near The Hague so they could capture Queen Wilhelmina, the Dutch government and the General Staff. Some French reinforcements arrived on 13 May but they weren't enough to hold back the dam. There was no little Dutch boy with a finger in a crack of the dyke holding back this evil tide.

The Germans attacked the Grebbe Line of defense, using our own Dutch POWs as human shields, letting them be killed as the Germans captured the line by the end of the day. Still, the German troops were stopped at Rotterdam, but as other areas were overrun, and there were no reserve troops, it soon became obvious that defeat was imminent. It was not soon enough for the Germans who wanted us out of their way. French and British troops couldn't get to us soon enough to make the necessary difference and save us from being conquered. The Germans would show us who was in control by annihilating Rotterdam.

Tired of the delays and heavy resistance near Rotterdam, on 14 May, Hitler ordered the German *Luftwaffe's* squadron of bombers to bomb Europe's largest port to smithereens. Rotterdam was only a little smaller than Amsterdam and the Rotterdam Blitz killed almost 900 people. We first heard that 40,000 had been killed and believed that for several days. The news devastated us as everyone in the Netherlands knew that the Germans would continue their reign of death and destruction. There would be no stopping their carnage. We were all terrified as we knew what the outcome would be. We knew they would not stop. I could tell Opa and my father were more than concerned for their families. There was a cold fear tightening around their hearts. I didn't realize until later how helpless they felt.

Later we learned that the bombs had destroyed the inner city of Rotterdam and left more than 78,000 people homeless. The Germans blackmailed our leaders by threatening to bomb our major cities of Utrecht, The Hague and even Amsterdam next if we didn't surrender. So, on 15 May, General Henri Winkelman, the Dutch commander, signed our surrender, except for Zeeland where French troops were helping us still. Zeeland surrendered four days later after the *Luftwaffe* bombed Middelburg. The French quickly retreated to help their own country which was also being invaded. Our leaders rightly determined that with the tremendous power of the German army, we couldn't take the risk of losing another of our major cities when it was obvious we could not win the War. Hitler used this tactic of *Schrecklichkeit* (frightfulness) and terror to break a country's will to resist. We would all know much more of his terror in the next years. Our leaders surrendered to save the rest of the population, not knowing the hardships of the slow death of our country and people over the next five years. Thankfully, none of us knew of the hardships coming our way or it would have overwhelmed us.

The Dutch people were shocked that Hitler had so blatantly lied and broken the agreement that he had affirmed time and again. The Dutch walked around in disbelief, stunned to the point of not being able to function for a few days, trying to grasp what had happened to our little country. It was especially horrific for German Jews who had fled to Holland, hoping this country would be a safe haven. Recognizing the evil that had just been unleashed on their new harbor, many frantically attempted to flee to other countries while they still could. They were desperate to get away from the Nazis for they knew what we didn't yet. Right after Holland surrendered, some 300 hopeless, realistic Jewish people committed suicide. In some instances, complete families killed themselves. A large percentage of them were German Jews who had already experienced Hitler's wrath in Germany. They just could not face again the brutality of his regime again. Some of us thought of them as the smart ones. They understood the unrestrained wickedness flowing onto our land and through much of Europe. They had saved their families and themselves untold grief and horror.

German forces continued their march and took France just a few days later. Soon we found out that Queen Wilhelmina and a few armed forces fled from The Hague by boat to Britain. Juliana and her family went on to Canada. We were alone. Our leaders were scattered, our forces beaten and the French troops had left to save their own country, but at least our Queen and her family were safe. It made us feel a little better that a very important part of us was still free. Queen Wilhelmina contacted her beloved people often throughout the next five years on the illegal Radio Oranje. The Resistance was quickly birthed on 15 May when, all alone, Bernard IJzerdraat passed out pamphlets in Rotterdam calling for the Dutch people to resist the Germans and immediately began the Resistance movement of the Beggars.

Hitler wasted no time. Within one week after Holland lost the fight to keep Germany from occupying our country, Hitler appointed one of his Austrian friends by the name of Arthur Seyss-Inquart as the *Reichskommissar*, the Supreme Ruler of Holland, for the Occupied Netherlands. He turned out to be the most fanatic anti-Jewish Nazi SS-officer Hitler could have selected. After the War, he was hanged for his reign of terror in our country, but while in control, he issued decrees, more decrees and decrees on top of decrees to control and destroy the Dutch Jews. The boa had us and our slow death had begun.

Seyss-Inquart took anti-Semitism to a new low in the next few years. He immediately began ruling by decrees, making

 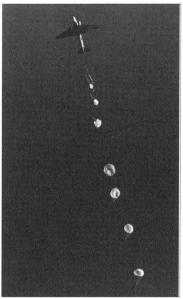

Newspaper with the awful headlines and German paratroopers dropped into our country (Photographs in Public Domain).

them the law of the land. First, he removed all Jews from the government, from the press and from any leadership positions in any industry. My father had served as a volunteer air-raid warden, but they kicked him out with all the Jews. In November, all 2,500 Jews were expelled from the Dutch Civil Service, including the Chief Justice of the Dutch Supreme Court and 41 university professors, although students and other professors protested. The last decree of 1940 was that all the Jewish businesses had to be registered. If businesses failed to register, the owners would be sent to jail and their businesses seized.

Decrees, rules, laws and restrictions defined Seyss-Inquart's reign. There were a lot of decrees right away that only applied to the Jews. After all, we were their main target. It was very hard on many of them, but on many of the Dutch citizenry there really wasn't much change. Remember our pluralism – things that affected Jews didn't affect many others because of the divisions.

Many of the same people were still in charge; mayors were the same, city councils and most provinces were still run pretty much the same, often with the same people in those offices. If you weren't a Jew or an undesirable, life really wasn't that bad for being occupied by the Nazis. Some thought we were treated better by the Germans because the Dutch were considered close "brothers" to the *Deutsch* (Germans), with many blonde haired, blue-eyed boys and girls running around Holland. Actually, our religious secularization made "real" Dutch people full-blooded Aryans. These Hollanders were already as close as you could get to being an Aryan race and the Nazis hoped they could convert our ideology over to theirs without too much work. Hitler actually wanted to absorb us into them and make our country part of Germany after the War, so he didn't want to kill off too many good Aryans, just the disgusting Jews.

When you consider how the Nazis took over Poland completely, as well as France and other countries, but left us to

German planes flew across our sky and dropped soldiers into our land (Photograph in Public Domain).

pretty much run ourselves, it seemed a possible reasoning for such actions. When the Germans took over Vienna, we heard stories about Jews forced down on their hands and knees to "scrub the streets clean from their filth." Our synagogues had not been burned down and we weren't being forced into ghettos, yet. We were living in denial, self-deluded that Hitler wasn't as bad as they had said and that we had dodged the bullet because we were close cousins to the Aryans and cooperating somewhat with them. At first, we convinced ourselves the occupation was just a temporary inconvenience and would soon be over. Surely things would go back to the way things always had been and we wouldn't have to change to their twisted ideology.

Their ideology was the problem. In Holland, before the War, there was a pro-Nazi movement that was supported from Berlin. It did not grow much because most of the Dutch

Destruction of Rotterdam (Photographs in Public Domain).

population did not embrace the violence and the racial ideology of this radical group. This was the National Socialist Movement in the Netherlands, *Nationaal-Socialistische Beweging* (NSB). Immediately after the invasion began, Dutch officials quickly jailed over 700 NSB members, rightly afraid of their loyalties. After the Netherlands surrendered and Seyss-

Inquart took power, he freed them all. He backed them up and supported this political party, giving them permission to form a paramilitary *Landwacht* (army) acting like an auxiliary police force in controlling the newly taken-over population. The NSB enjoyed their new power and used it to bully, hurt and destroy the Jews of their own country.

These Dutch men, "friends and neighbors," were strong sympathizers with the Germans and openly collaborated with them. Their membership grew to over 100,000 as some of the weaker Dutch quickly changed sides to whoever had the power. Anton Mussert was our country's chief Nazi collaborator and leader of the NSB during the 1930's and 1940's. Hitler even called him the "Fuehrer of the Netherlands" though he had

1940 - Dutch negotiator and troops surrender to Nazis
(Photograph in Public Domain).

little real power. These men took to their jobs with gusto and enjoyed their newfound power, often being much crueler to the Dutch Jews than the Germans were. They turned on all of us that they described as "filthy undesirables." Although we had heard the stories from many of the German Jews, we could not fathom that we, too, little by little, would be cruelly robbed of our humanity and suffer degradation not ever meant for a person made in the image of Yahweh.

Although the Netherlands was occupied, not all was lost. The colonies were still free for a time, but Japan would invade them soon. Queen Wilhelmina and the Dutch government were operating out of London. Most of the ships of the Royal Netherlands Navy had gotten to England and our merchant marine helped out in the Allied war effort. Even a few Dutch pilots had escaped and joined the Royal Air Force of Britain. We were occupied, but our people were not beaten down yet. The day after our capitulation, the first Dutch Resistance

Dutch bicycle Troops on 14 May.
(Photograph in Public Domain).

organization met. The Germans occupied our land, but they did not own us.

All of us heard stories of Dutch citizens, Jews and others who had "gotten away." Many of us regretted our "bad luck." Those of us left in Holland paid huge emotional, physical, psychological and spiritual prices – beyond any humans' capability to comprehend. All of this made my mind tired. I just wanted to sit and watch the ships and not think of what had happened and what was happening to my whole life and to the people I loved.

In December, we looked forward to Sinterklaas, so that finally something close to normal talk took place. Plus, my birthday

Queen Wilhelmina in Amsterdam before the War (Photograph in Public Domain) and Arthur Seyss-Inquart, the Supreme Ruler of Holland after we capitulated (United States Holocaust Memorial Museum).

Two days later, the Germans drive on Raadhuisstraat in Amsterdam 16 May 1940 in victory (Photograph in Public Domain).

was coming up and that always made it an even more special time for me. Maybe Sinterklaas' visit and my fourteenth birthday would get things back on an even keel. About five days or so before December 5, children would put out their shoes at night in front of their fireplace or stove, tuck some straw and maybe a few carrots for Sinterklaas' horse in our shoes and hope we had been deemed a good child. If we were, Sinterklaas (or our parents) would put a tiny gift in one of the shoes and we would be thrilled. None of us ever wanted the piece of coal because we had not been a good child.

(Talking about carrots, here is an aside for you in why carrots are orange. In the 17th century, Dutch growers cultivated a mixture of the white and red carrots into orange as a tribute to William of Orange for leading the struggle for our Dutch independence. So now, most carrots are descended from the Horn Carrot, bred in the town of Hoorn. So, think of us Dutch next time you have your carrots.)

Our celebration was wonderful, even though we still had not

Dutch volunteers join the Waffen-SS (photosofwwii.com).
Shame on all of them.

completely rebounded from the Great Depression. I had never known a large, extravagant holiday so I thought this one was bountiful. We had a few fresh fruits, whittled gifts, presents with little verses attached, bright candles, cookies, a pot of wonderful hot chocolate and, of course, a visit from Sinterklaas or St. Nicholas, Amsterdam's patron saint.

Opa and Oma had traveled up from Zandvoort to stay with us for a few days. Opa brought some of his fresh baked *bok-kepootjes* (cookies with pieces of sugared ginger) and Oma brought her delicious homemade candies and *poffertje* (mini-pancakes). Opa, Father, Leo and I perched up on one of the higher streets above the harbor and watched the Bishop (Sinterklaas) with his servant, Peter, the black Moor, disembark from the big ship that brought him on 5 December. He then rode his beautiful white horse through the streets of *de Rivierenbuurt*, a river neighborhood. This was a festive time and we enjoyed the break from the grumpiness of not knowing

Occupied (Photograph in Public Domain).

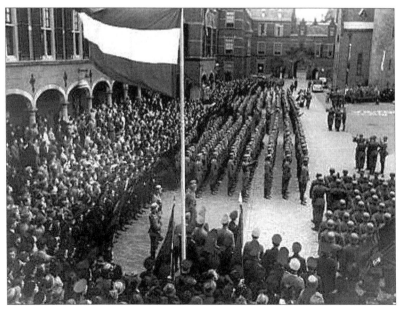

*Dutch volunteers enter the German army
(Photograph in Public Domain).*

41

*Occupying Germans take Amsterdam and all of Holland
(Photograph in Public Domain).*

*Map of the
Netherlands/
Holland
(Photograph in
Public Domain).*

our future. This normal activity was heartwarming, just to hear and to join in laughter with family closeness.

This year, my father had hired a man to come as Sinterklaas to our home. He came in all jolly and laughing, then asked if all the children had been good boys and girls. Of course we all yelled, *"Jah"* to being good and then he threw candy on the floor, which all of us would immediately rush to get. Part of the payment for the Sinterklaas, at every home he visited, was a shot of gin. By the time our Sinterklaas got to our home, he was snookered. Being drunk though, he was still very joyful and happy and Opa, Father and a few other friends and relatives thought it very amusing. It was a wonderful time and one of the last times all my family was together and safe. In the coming years, my mind would often go back to this time of joy and I would escape to this safe place in my *koph*, almost tasting the cookies and candy again.

Chapter Three: 1941

In the second week of January, when I was just 14, the Nazis showed us early on what this year would be like. They issued a sweeping decree on 10 January that all Jews were ordered to officially register themselves with their town's Registrar. Everyone had to be fingerprinted and photographed. Forms had to be filled out with our total personal history, names, dates, relatives, addresses and answers to questions like, "Do you have any Jewish grandparents?" Not to register was punished by five years in jail. Very few Jews, less than 50, did not register and by the end, 140,000 Jews were registered across our country. This registration turned out to be a disaster because now the Germans, with the help of Dutch workers, drew up maps, identified the names, genders, ages, marital

43

status and locations of all Jews living in every Dutch city and town. They knew where every Jew lived and later, this would make it easy to arrest us and round us up for "resettlement" and ultimately murder most of us. The Jews were cornered and we were finally comprehending much more what that really meant.

Things kept ramping up for the worse in Holland. Arthur Seyss-Inquart continued his fanatic drive against the Dutch Jews. This man with the crippled leg was determined to destroy all Jews in the Netherlands. In February, Seyss-Inquart, whose mind was really what was crippled, completely sealed off Amsterdam's Hebrew quarter and established Jewish ghettos, locking Jews away from other humans, isolating and controlling them in a place called the *"Juden viertel"* (Jewish quarter) or *"Joodsche wijk"* (Jewish neighborhood).

Our family still lived in a middle-class neighborhood because my mother was not Jewish, but other Jews weren't so fortunate. Our country had been invaded by the Germans and they now forced most Jews to be confined in their own neighborhoods, only they weren't called neighborhoods, but were called Jewish ghettos. The Nazis didn't want the hassle with governing the ghettos, so on 13 February, they appointed a Jewish council (the Judenrat). They really didn't have any power, but they had to make some gut-wrenching decisions between terrible and worse. The Rabbis and Jewish leaders distributed what little food there was, policed the ghettos and watched out for the "health and welfare" of the Jewish people imprisoned there. Without adequate food, medicine or sanitation this was a losing battle. Jews were already dying at alarming rates and that was exactly what the Nazis wanted. The Jewish council did whatever they could to save lives, but the frustration they felt in every single thing they did was debilitating.

Sealed ghettos meant those tight packed areas within a city

that were closed off, walled off or enclosed with barbed wire. In Amsterdam, the canals acted as built-in barriers and the bridges were natural "gates" to the ghettos. Jews in the ghettos were no longer free to come and go as they pleased. In fact, any Jew caught leaving the ghetto could be shot. People lived where the Nazis told you to live and as more Jews from around Holland were forced into Amsterdam, people would be shoe-horned into apartments with others and everyone better shut up and put up with it. People only got food at the times the Germans told them they were allowed to get it and whatever they got was limited to what and how much you would be allowed to have.

Ghettos cut off the prisoners by brick walls or barbed wire. For people within the ghetto, it was a crazy quilt of ghetto boundaries, extremely crowded and extremely unsanitary. Food was always in short supply and many Jews slowly starved

LEFT: Sinterklaas and the Moor walk the streets of Amsterdam (Photograph in Public Domain).
RIGHT: Sinterklaas, the Moor and his beautiful white horse (Holland.com).

to death. Energy for heat and cooling was sporadic, inadequate and almost non-existent, especially as the War went on year after year. With this many people stuffed into such close quarters, diseases such as dysentery and typhus were epidemic, swelling the mortality rate. Still, the death numbers were not high enough for Hitler. Every day, each ghetto had a somber procession of taking the dead bodies to their mass graves.

Part of the reason we were so naïve is that we didn't expect the Nazis to ramp up so quickly, but that was their purpose. They immediately started doing what they had been doing in Germany and Poland for several years already. We just didn't comprehend. There were many of us who saw German trucks and troops going by on roads, but we didn't realize what they were doing because we were cut off from each other. There were people starving to death blocks away from us, but because of the way the ghetto was isolated from what could be called daily life, the ghettos were horrible secret death traps. There were many people in the cities who did not really know the devastation going on right next to them.

When you think about it, Jews represented less than 10% of Amsterdam's total population. As Holland's largest city, it had a Jewish population which had ballooned to more than 84,000 when Jews from around Europe came here for refuge. Later, as Jews from the country and villages were rounded up and forced into Amsterdam's ghetto, the overcrowding was insufferable. As the ghettos expanded Amsterdam's Jewish population to about 100,000, most of them were soon deported to the death camps in Poland.

Ghettos were engineered to be horrible, depriving Jews of food, medical care and any other basics needed for bare survival, including heating or water. Lice, fleas and bed bugs were rampant. Starvation rations were all our people received. Conditions inside the ghettos were cramped, miserable and deadly. Most SS-run ghettos were totally inadequate for the people they imprisoned. The ghettos had insufficient housing, shelter, water and sewage facilities for all inhabitants. The greatest physical danger in the ghettos came not from the Nazis per se, but from starvation and disease. The quantity and quality of food was pitiful: most meals consisted of watery soups, some brewed with a few beans or grains, others with straw or grass. Hell had come to Holland.

When all this was combined, such deprivation couldn't help but produce sickness and epidemics, including typhus and other contagious diseases which were common. Jews were used as slave labor by the Germans in the cities, often dying of malnutrition, disease or starvation. They were executed for "crimes" or shot just because they were Jews and the officers just felt like killing them. Sanitary conditions were deplorable, food and good drinking water were hard to come by because ghetto Jews were only allowed to buy food during certain hours and there wasn't much, if any, left after "real" people bought

Workers at offices of Joodshe Raad (Jewish Council) in Amsterdam (holocaustresearchproject.org). Sign to the Judenrat (Jewish Council) in Amsterdam (Photograph in Public Domain).

their supplies. The Germans counted on disease, starvation or malnutrition and wretched conditions to kill off the Jewish population and they weren't disappointed.

As the Jews kept dying, the Germans pushed their lies so that "normal" people would "realize" that the Germans were right in destroying the filthy Jews. One film forcibly had to be shown in every town and every theater across Holland and the rest of Europe: "The Eternal Jew." This disgusting film, made in Germany, depicted Jews like dirty rats, overtaking the streets of every town and village. It fostered fear and loathing of Jews in every single occupied country. The Germans made it more powerful by inserting local material into the film about the plague of rats (Jews) overrunning good people's lives. This film made it a lot easier for the Germans in their local propaganda; many non-Jews fell for the lies, causing much extra hardship on the Jews.

In the next few years, the ghettos would be emptied and destroyed as the "Final Solution" got closer to accomplishment. Himmler wanted the ghettos emptied by early 1944. Emptied

Signs read, "Jewish quarter" in German and "Jewish neighborhood" in Dutch – across the bridge (Photograph in Public Domain and United States Holocaust Memorial Museum).

meant all those Jews gone and exterminated. Throughout this year of 1941, Jews still didn't believe that the Nazis were killing them. They really thought it was all about resettlement and all would turn out alright. The mind is a strange thing and many could not fathom the reality of their dire situation.

The stop gap of the ghettos was relieved of some of its overcrowding as Jews were shipped indirectly or directly to the concentration camps. What we found unbelievable was that after the War, many Dutch people didn't even realize what we Jews were going through because much of it did not directly affect them. So here we were, many of us dying and being shipped off to our deaths and yet our neighbors and countrymen often didn't understand the extent of our suffering. Some people just denied that such atrocities could happen in their country and lived as if nothing was going on. It is a good lesson for all of us to pay attention to our governments and what freedoms they take away from any of us.

The way Amsterdam was built, segregation and confinement of the Jews to the ghettos was a relatively easy operation, blocking us off from other areas of the city; the four major canals and then other canals blocked off areas from other

Ghetto poverty's soup line (United States Holocaust Memorial Museum).
Bridge leading to Jewish Quarter of Amsterdam
(holocaustresearchproject.org).

49

areas. The Batavians settled Amsterdam and built the canals for protection. Now the Nazis used them to lock us Jews up; Germans controlled the bridges and kept us where they wanted us to stay. Jews were as the plague to many of them.

Our own engineering of our city made it easy for our captors to shut Jews away by closing bridges and canals to keep us where they wanted us. Except this winter, unlike others, the cold was severe enough to freeze some of the canals and many Jews would slip out to the country and find some food. There was no light afternoon ice skating or races on such canals as had been done for many years. Now the race was to outlive the Germans and their death camps.

There were basically three Jewish quarters in Amsterdam, one in the Center, one in Amsterdam East and one in Amsterdam South. When the Germans wanted to control the Jews, they closely guarded the bridges, used barbed wire and determined who would and could go where and when from the cramped ghettos. Keeping Jews from other Jews as isolation added more fear to the equation. Once they had Jews segregated and confined in the Amsterdam ghettos, it was easy to make demands from them and control them basically with extreme fear. Besides they wouldn't be around long if they had their way – they wanted them shipped out to the death camps. It was all part of Hitler's systematic extermination of the Jews and other *untermenschen* (less than humans).

Black shirted NSB (Nationaal-Socialistische Beweging; also referred to as National Socialist Movement members/ volunteers that wore black shirts to symbolize their support of the movement) members enjoyed bullying Jews. In mid-February, a bunch of NSB thugs went into a working-class neighborhood, marched into an ice cream parlor and forced all the Jews out into the street and brutally beat them. NSB harassed the Jews and bullied them unmercifully. There were a few Jewish people who fought back in self defense at this time. A Dutch Nazi was killed and a Gestapo soldier was injured. In reprisal over the next two days, the Germans arrested 425 Jewish men, women and children, who were right away transported to the concentration camps of Buchenwald first and then to Mauthausen. Within three months, almost all were dead. The families of these Jews received their death notices. The camp of Mauthausen would remain a synonym for death. Mauthausen was located near Linz, Austria, Hitler's home in his early youth. Now it was known only for its death.

After the War, I visited Mauthausen myself and would like to tell you something about this camp. It is located on top of a hill next to a granite quarry. To build the camp, the prisoners had to build a stairway of 300 steps going up the hill. After building the stairway, the prisoners cut blocks of granite and carried them on their shoulders up the steps. In this fashion, they built this whole concentration camp. Many Jews and prisoners died just building the camp.

Jews separated from "normal" citizens (histclo.com).

51

The camp also had a chamber where the Nazis did incomprehensible medical experiments on prisoners. As I was reading the names of the people who died in the camp, I found six names of my relatives, including some Van Gelders from my father's side. In my visit to the quarry, I was able to pick up a piece of granite which I brought home as a memory and show it to people so they understand the hardships those people went through.

The NSB thugs and the arrests and brutality of the Nazis against Jews protecting themselves sparked a huge response in the Dutch citizenry. The Dutch Communist/Workers Party - a political party already deemed illegal by the Nazis but still operating within the Netherlands with 15% of the population as members - organized what has become known as the February Strike. On Tuesday, 25 February, municipal workers of Amsterdam went on strike *(staakt!)* in defense of the Jews, essentially shutting down public transportation within the city – all trams stopped. The Dutch citizenry was angry at what the

Poster advertising the "Eternal Jew" (United States Holocaust Memorial Museum).

Germans had done to the Jews. They were stunned, bewildered, frustrated and mad. Remember, the Netherlands had not been actively in a war since the days of Napoleon and we didn't like our people being killed.

Over the course of the day, the strike expanded and intensified into mass demonstrations as metal and shipyard workers, white collar workers, major factory workers, manual laborers and most public servants joined the strike. Thousands marched in columns along the Rozengracht to the center of Amsterdam, singing "Internationale" as a form of unity. The strike continued until Thursday, spreading across the country to other cities. These wonderful Dutch Gentiles still thought that they could dissuade the Germans from their evil pathway. The

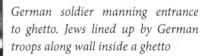

German soldier manning entrance to ghetto. Jews lined up by German troops along wall inside a ghetto

(Photographs in Public Domain).

53

This aerial photo of Amsterdam shows the grid and the four major curved canals. From the outside to the inside, you can remember them as PKHS, Please Kiss Her Softly: Prinsen Gracht, Keizers Gracht, Heren Gracht and Singel (Photograph in Public Domain).

infuriated Nazis struck back hard, brutally squashing the strike, executing the leaders and promising a bloodbath. It remains the only anti-German strike to have occurred in Nazi-occupied Europe. The workers were soon forced to accept the truth of the Germans' goal to destroy Jews, all Jews, and they wouldn't allow anyone or anything to get in their way.

I am not sure if they still get together, but for many years, people would gather in the Jonas Daniel Meijerplein. The large group stood in front of a statue of a dockworker, to commemorate and be thankful for that strike. This was not a strike like so many other strikes or protests. This one was where Dutch men and women revolted against the brutality of the Nazis' horrific treatment of us Jews. For that, we Jews will always be thankful.

After the defiance shown by the Amsterdam unions, the Germans quit any pretense at being nice or conciliatory with any of us Dutch. Three mayors who had been lenient with the strikers were yanked out of office and replaced by Dutch Nazis from the NSB. More NSB members were put into places of power and, even though they didn't control the country, they acted like it. They became more and more aggressive in their wicked actions toward all the Dutch Jews especially. Bullying confrontations became normal occurrences. They sauntered around in their black shirted gangs, routinely beating up and sometimes killing Jewish or other "sub-human" people; just because they could and no one in authority would stop them. All Nazi Germans were preparing for their larger German Empire and no one would get in their way.

Decrees came fast and furious after this encounter. On 13 March, there was a decree for "the removal of all Jews from economic life." Any leftover Jews were "dismissed" from any public office. Jews were segregated from other Dutchmen,

Dutch Nazi party members stand in the doorway of a restaurant (holocaustresearch project.org).

banned from cafes, parks and other public gathering places. Signs banning Jews were everywhere either in Dutch or German to make us know the Nazis now owned our country and our language. Unfortunately, there were no more solidarity strikes as the Nazis had forced the fear down the Dutch' peoples throats and into the lives of normal Dutch citizens. Jews were the marked ones and it was made very clear that it was in the "normal" citizens' interest not to help us in any way. We were off limits to "normal" people.

During the spring, anti-Jewish measures got even worse for all of us with decree after decree. Starting in April, all Jews were forbidden to enter hotels, restaurants, movie theaters and even a bench on the street had a sign on it, *Joden niet gewenst*, "No Jews allowed" - on a bench along the street, for pity sakes! I couldn't swim in the public pool, sit on a bench in a public park or go to a restaurant with my family, but there was no decree stating that I could not go sailing on a boat on the Amstel, but it didn't matter because no one would rent a boat to a Jew. I had a small sailboat, but did not push that limit.

On 1 May, strict limitations were decreed for our employment. About now, too, all Jews were forced to give up their radios, which had to be in good working condition or we had to pay for repairs! This impacted all Jews negatively because hundreds of thousands of us listened to the Dutch Oranje radio from London. Now we would not have any true information, only the lies of the Germans. Many Dutch people hid their radios. We needed to know what was real. Many turned to the Resistance as necessary to inform all of us Dutch what was truth. The Resistance also used their forgery skills and made ration books and stole to feed people in hiding.

Up until now, the Jewish children were spared from the Nazi decrees. This came to an end, too, when it was announced that with the start of the new school year Jewish children were not

Mauthausen front gates and stairs of death as prisoners carry stones from the quarry to build the concentration camp (Photographs in Public Domain).

permitted in "Aryan" schools or public schools.

With this change in the way Jewish children would be educated, Jews were forced to open special schools for the Jewish children only. Most parents did not let their children go to these schools for fear that they would be raided by the German Nazis and their children taken. I had finished 6th

Prisoners labor in the quarry
(United States Holocaust Memorial Museum) and (Bundesarchive).

grade, but now my parents decided to keep me out of school. I would help my father in the factory where his employees made decorative accessories like fancy tablecloths, tea cozies and other interior-design merchandise. We were not sure how much longer we would be able to keep this new normal that was not at all normal.

Nothing was normal in our lives and one evening, something very abnormal happened. The door bell rang and when I opened the door, a *Luftwaffe* officer (German Air Force) was standing there, asking me if "Uncle Levie" was home. I knew enough to be frightened when I first saw him, but then for him to call my father "Uncle Levie" was not at all normal. I quickly called to my father and when he saw this officer, he got all excited. It turned out that my father, during the years that he had worked as a buyer for a textile company and went to Germany to work, had become good friends with the father of this officer. After a couple of visits, this officer was telling my father that he was part of bombing London, but that this was totally against his conscience because he was not a Nazi believer and wanted to stop doing what he was doing.

He kept visiting us, but after a while, Father was forced to tell him that the neighbors were getting suspicious and would turn us in. Then the officer asked my father if he could help get him some civilian clothing because he wanted to desert the German services. My father said in doing so, the whole family

Mauthausen corpses strewn around the grounds, shown after liberation (United States Holocaust Memorial Museum).

could be killed. However, Father also said that he could not help it if somebody would steal clothing from a chair in the front room. So after that there was one more visit from him and the clothing was stolen from the chair. After the War, my father was complimented for this work for the Underground.

And the decrees kept coming against us Jews. The next decree across Holland changed life for my grandparents and was the beginning of their end. The decree was that all Jews living in beach and resort towns were forced to leave their homes and

*The Dutch strike against treatment of Jews in Amsterdam
(United States Holocaust Memorial Museum).*

move to Amsterdam. Work was expanding on the Atlantic Wall fortifications and workers needed to put in more time and labor and some towns were dismantled As you know from earlier in my book, my grandparents were retired and working in the beautiful beach town of Zandvoort where Leo and I used to go to visit during the summers.

Now, they were forced to sell their comfortable home and business for almost nothing. They came to Amsterdam and moved in above us in a small apartment of two rooms and a small kitchen. We were just grateful that the apartment above us was empty and they could move in so close to us. Much was lost. There would be no more enjoyable trips on our bicycles for Leo and me to our beloved grandparents' home. It was very traumatic for them, at their age, to make this move and to have lost so much of their worldly wealth and legacy for their children after their years and years of toil. Although they handled it seemingly well, it was a difficult time for all.

There was limited transportation for Jews since last year the Germans had sealed all petrol and most cars were converted to generators. I was told by my father to drive our large, 8 foot long

Bakfiets (tricycle cart) which we owned from our factory, with a big flat box in front of it to Zandvooort to pick up my grandparents' belongings. Since the town was about 25 miles from Amsterdam, it was a tough job to peddle down there and back and I did this about four times. Still my grandparents had lost much and were devastated. They had worked their whole lives to live somewhat comfortably and to be able to help their children. Now they were forced into a tiny apartment, confined with us by the Nazis, knowing it was difficult on everyone to even have enough food, let alone anything of a little luxury.

Because food was in short supply, sometimes I would go out to the farmers and barter things for some fresh vegetables, but it was getting harder and harder to accomplish unless you could get things from the Black Market. About now, the Germans closed my father's manufacturing plant and many other Jewish businesses. So now my father and mother had no jobs and no money. My father had already started operating within the Black Market and now he really expanded his involvement. He had many contacts and was very much involved in that Black Market and helped us and many others get through this difficult time. Fairness wasn't working and the food shortages

"No Jews" signs were posted in stores, on benches and in parks often in German to prove their power over us (Photographs in Public Domain).

soon gave an unfair advantage to whoever had money. During the War, the price of potatoes had gone over the roof. In Amsterdam and other areas of the country, there were food riots. People were beginning to get desperate and we had not even seen the worst yet.

Some saw me as just a boy, but my responsibilities were changing. I was given manly duties and responsibilities to help my beloved grandparents through this difficult time, to help my father and to help my mother bring food to family and friends who were hiding from the Nazis. Already, my carefree boyhood seemed long ago – except for sometimes outside of Amsterdam, where I wasn't always reminded of the occupation. Sometimes on my trips through the country to the coast, it was almost like the good old days! In fact, a funny thing was that I used a small sail (off my sail canoe since we weren't allowed on the lakes or canals anymore) and we mounted it on top of this tricycle and sailed like that down the road. A reporter of a newspaper saw me and took a picture and I landed up in the newspaper with my sailing tricycle! My innovation was helpful and newsworthy.

*Germans herding Jewish people for deportation
(United States Holocaust Memorial Museum
and holocaustresearchproject.org).*

Tricycle (bakfiets) similar to the one I rode around Amsterdam and to Zandvoort to pick up my grandparents' things (Photograph in Public Domain).

Swastikas and Nazi graffiti on an exterior wall of a synagogue in Amsterdam – notice tricycle like mine (holocaustresearchproject.org)

Bunkers near Zandvoort along Atlantic Wall (Photographs in Public Domain).

At this time I was 14 years old and out of a job because my father's factory had been closed. In Holland it was the legal age that you were allowed to have a job and so I got myself a job with a book store. On the tricycle, I improvised the large box in front of me by putting shelves on both sides for holding the books: westerns, romances and adventures. With this tricycle, I would go up and down the streets, ringing doorbells and people would come down and select a book and pay 10 cents for a week's rent. I would come back the next week to exchange for new books. And of course, as long as it was not raining, it was alright. This was Holland and I spent a lot of time wet.

One day on my way back to the store, I was passing the old age home for the Jewish people. There was a row of German army trucks loading all the people into the trucks. Some walked, some hobbled on crutches, and some were unable to walk and were in wheelchairs. As I was watching them load truck after truck until the home was empty, I realized how great someone's hate must be to take all those Jews who were old,

Jews seized in their homes are brought by truck to railroad stations for deportation (holocaustresearchproject.org) and the Jewish Hospital in Amsterdam (Yad Vashem.org).

feeble, and decrepit, then to move them on the pretense that they would be resettled in Theresienstadt. We found out later that all of them were murdered in concentration camps. It was one of those things that would come back into my mind over

Arrival of transport of Dutch Jews in the Theresienstadt ghetto (holocaustresearchproject.org). Jews moving along to be deported (United States Holocaust Memorial Museum).

and over again – those old people being shoved along, stuffed into trucks like cattle and hauled away to their deaths.

For my job of renting out books, I was cycling all over Amsterdam and the ghettos and middle-class neighborhoods. A few days after watching the elderly trucked away, one of my customers was all flustered as he told me that someone had told him that the Germans were underway to empty the Jewish hospital. So as fast as I could peddle, I drove down in the rain and when I arrived there the staff was wheeling all of the patients out of the building on anything that would move. Once outside, they were to await the German trucks coming to load up the people. Now I knew what would happen to these people and I was determined not to stand by and watch it happen again without me doing something to stop it. I was my mother's son after all.

There were already other Dutch patriots there, whisking

LEFT: Carre Theatre is on the left. My father's sister (my aunt) lived in one of those front apartments.
RIGHT: Kloveniersburgwal (Photographs by Charles Breijer in collection of Nederlands Fotomuseum).

Arrested Jews in Amsterdam (memorialmuseums. net). Amsterdam Jews thought they were being resettled and even got dressed up for their trip (Photograph in Public Domain).

patients away from the hospital. To help the patients flee, I would, with the help of other people, lift 3 or 4 patients at a time on the top of the box on my tricycle and I would peddle those patients about six or seven blocks away where other people would help to lift them down, quickly moving them away into apartments and then I would drive back to get more. I was able to save about 30 patients. When the German trucks arrived, they found the whole hospital empty of patients and staff. They were very angry and, if it hadn't been raining really hard, probably would have stayed and found out more from the neighbors. It was a wonderful feeling of helping snatch those people to safety after the horror of watching what had happened to the people in the old people's home when I felt so helpless as they were trucked away to their deaths.

It wasn't just the old and the physically unfit who were targeted. Later, the Germans put into place their plan of deportation by sending letters at random to Jewish families that they would be transported to Theresienstadt to "start a new life." At that time, many Jews still believed this lie and got ready to travel with just a suitcase or duffel bag of clothes, because that was all they were allowed to take. Within their pockets or linings of clothing, they would hide their jewelry. It was taken right away, supposedly to be stored for later and to be given back after they arrived, which of course never happened. Much of what had been promised never happened. Many never went to Theresienstadt and were directly transported to Auschwitz or other camps where, upon arrival, the family would be split up and divided to confuse and frighten them.

At this time in Auschwitz, most prisoners were executed by firing squads, but it was expensive and inefficient. The murderous Germans began experimenting with carbon monoxide as a quicker extermination because some of the SS troops were wearing out physically and emotionally from

LEFT: Underground cover of Yiddish newspaper (United States Holocaust Memorial Museum)

LOWER: hideout from Nazis (Photograph in Public Domain).

manually killing all those people in cold blood. To make the killers' jobs easier, they experimented with carbon monoxide and would attach the exhausts of trucks to rooms and kill the prisoners that way. Later, they graduated to Zyklon B gas pellets for an even faster genocide.

I must repeat, of the 140,000 Jews registered and living in the Netherlands in early 1940, estimations range that only 20,000 to 30,000 survived the War. Less than a quarter of the Jews in Amsterdam survived the War. It is important to understand why the death toll was so high. The Dutch civil records were excellent, having recorded substantial information on every Dutch national. It was relatively easy for the Gestapo to access

jews arrested in Amsterdam (Photograph in Public Domain) and ready for deportation (AnneFrank House).

Amsterdam Jews led off for deportation and likely death (holocaustresearchproject.org).

this information and easily determine who was Jewish because of the registration. Still, even as thousands died by genocide, many Jews were in denial about what was happening to themselves, their families, and their race. They wanted to believe that the Nazis weren't systematically exterminating them. At the beginning of WWII, the Nazis eliminated many of the intelligentsia and religious leaders, leaving the rest of the Jewish population without strong, knowledgeable leadership or genuine news. Our people were led as sheep to the slaughter.

Now, you ask why the Jews went without much questioning. Place yourself into this period of time with no communications. You would hear news only on "illegal" radios or read it in newspapers which were controlled by the Germans. Every day you would hear those men in uniform boasting about how fantastic they were and how the German Reich was helping our country. Other than that, the only things you would hear were rumors. Normal, sane people could not fathom the horrific atrocities committed by humans on other humans as they were stripped of their humanity. Many could not make their minds go there.

Much later in the War, when the Underground papers came out, some of the terrible stories of the concentration camps filtered through. The Germans sent out death notices of people who had left Holland. In fear of what was happening, some Jews tried to "buy" their loved ones' ways out of Dachau and a few other concentration camps. They had to have the tickets to their destination, often Shanghai, in hand and a "sponsor" in that other country. Many went to Argentina, too. People would wait for hours and even days in line to get their tickets and then travel to the concentration camp to free their loved one. The Germans just wanted the Jews gone. However, this system of letting the Jews leave the country ended later because it was too much paper work. It was easier just to annihilate them.

71

Every day there was more bad news, more horror stories. People were in shock over their horrible circumstances and the ghastly things that were happening. Many people suffered from depression with some never coming out of it. Many of the Jewish casualties of the War were Jews who were still alive, but emotionally and/or physically crippled. If you've seen the movie, "Sophie's Choice," you have a sense of the emotional devastation that followed WWII victims for years and years; and Sophie wasn't even a Jew. Many of us thought that the Nazis would never hurt children. We were so very wrong. It was estimated that only one in ten Jewish children in Europe survived the War.

All Jews were barred from having any membership in any organization that was not Jewish. All professional people were out of work because they were not allowed to have non-Jewish customers. Jews couldn't afford the Gentiles' services and products. There were no jobs and all the Jews were sliding into poverty. So when the Germans requested people for labor in Germany, many figured that they had no other choice and it would help their families. After they received their notices to work as laborers, they would present themselves at *De Hollandsche Schouwburg* Theatre in Amsterdam for transport. I, myself, brought many families there with my tricycle. They would go there with nothing but their rucksacks with a few clothes and valuables, hoping they would survive their resettlement. Many really didn't comprehend their futures.

At this time, the Nazis would pick up the Jews at this Jewish theater, which had been just an ordinary theater before the War. Now, it was used as the place where Jews would assemble before being trucked off by the Nazis to concentration or labor camps. It was always cramped and packed. The only place to get some air was in the courtyard. While waiting for transports to come and take them away, children 12 and under were grabbed from their families and put into a day care center across the street until the whole family was transported out. *De Hollandsche Schouwburg* Theatre in Amsterdam was often a Jew's last stop before some type of death.

Death, fear and suffering were dominant across the Netherlands and, personally, my family was also going through difficulties. My brother, Leo, was a well-known concert pianist and schooled at the Amsterdam Bach Conservatory from which he finished cum laude. His job at that time was playing the piano and harmonica in bars and dance schools. While Leo was working in those places to earn a living, he met a Jewish girl in one of the dance schools. Her name was Jetty and she became his girlfriend. She was 17 years of age.

Now, you must know what was going on with the Germans. Jews had figured out what *De Hollandsche Schouwburg* Theatre in Amsterdam meant and wouldn't go there as easily. The Germans still used it as a gathering place for those going into forced labor. To get people to the concentration camps, the Nazis would swoop into neighborhoods and pick up Jews at their homes or walking down the streets, shipping them off to concentration camps. A Jew could be walking to a neighbor's home, be picked up and never be seen again. Fear was everywhere.

Let me explain the difficult experiences of this young woman who became a heroine of mine. Jetty's parents died when she was very young and she was an orphan living with her uncle and aunt who raised her. While she was dating Leo, one day she was working as she normally did, and something terrible happened to her and changed her life forever. She came home from work and, during that particular day, the Germans had conducted a raid in her neighborhood of the Jewish Ghetto. The Gestapo arrested Jetty's Uncle and Aunt and they were sent to a concentration camp and never returned. The Germans had sealed Jetty's home and confiscated all furnishings and belongings. They would ship all this to Germany. On the side of the trains it would say, "A winter gift from Holland." If anyone was found rummaging around in empty Jewish apartments, they were shot.

So here Jetty was, standing on the street with only the clothes she had on. She called Leo who came to get her and brought her to our home. My parents decided right away that she would move in with us to live. Sometimes there can also be some humor to a problem. Jetty was sleeping on a Murphy bed in the front room while my brother and I were sleeping in a room back toward the middle of the house. (A Murphy bed folded back into the wall and was covered by a curtain during the day.) The back of the house was connected by a long hallway to the front room. My brother would sneak down that hallway to make out with Jetty. One night they were in bed and the Murphy bed broke down and they were caught. We still laugh about that. My parents decided since they were not allowed to get married according to the Germans' decrees, my parents would allow them to sleep together the rest of the War, which they did. They got married after the War when the Germans no longer had any say over our lives.

Yes, this was Jetty's story, but this was many Jews' stories. Every single day, hundreds of Jews in Amsterdam would just disappear. The Gestapo would quickly surround a block, search house by house and grab any Jews they could find, stick them on trucks and deport them. Jetty came home from work, but many children came home from school and their parents were not only gone, but so were their homes. Often other Jews would take them in, but this, too, would be another danger added to just the all consuming dangers of being Jewish.

No one knew when these raids would come and where. One day, there was a lot of screaming in our backyard and we went out to see what was going on. We didn't even realize a raid

74

*Children deported from Westerbork
transit camp and Jewish children
liberated from Auschwitz (United
States Holocaust Memorial Museum).
Liberating American soldier looks
upon children buried in mass grave
(Photograph in Public Domain).
Children forced to haul wagon and
liberated boy from Auschwitz (United
States Holocaust Memorial Museum).*

was happening on our block. To our horror, a Jewish neighbor was hanging out of the third story window of his building, trying to escape the German soldiers in the building, but after a while, he could no longer hold on and fell to his death. It was a terrible experience. In some ways it was a blessing for him because he would have been sent to a concentration camp where executions were commonplace and most inmates were simply worked to death. Many Jews called any death outside the concentration camps a "good death."

Life in the ghettos was progressively so horrible that many would volunteer for "evacuation," because they would get an extra ration of bread. Many said that one more hour of life was still life. Long lines of starving Jews were ordered to enter the cattle cars of trains, usually more than 100 to each car. There was no air and if someone fainted, the packed conditions would keep the person standing up. Sanitary conditions were deplorable. There could be as many as 50 cattle cars to a train, as Jews were transported to death camps. Most of these victims were unaware of their ultimate destination because the Nazis used terms such as "evacuation" or "resettlement to the East." In later years, as a few Jews escaped from the death camps, the truth leaked out about the fate of all those Jews who were deported for "resettlement." Most Jews were sent to concentration or death camps where they were murdered one way or another. There was no resettlement, only death. What a travesty.

More rumors and stories came out about the concentration camps, two of which were the KZ Herzogenbusch near Vught and Kamp Amersfoort near Amersfoort. There was also, of course, the Westerbork transit camp where many Dutch Jews were sent before being deported to death camps. Later in the War, the Nazis didn't even bother pretending there was resettlement as they just sent Jews straight to the death camps to exterminate them. It was no wonder that stories of the concentration camps got out and brought deep dread and fear across

Hollandsche Schouwburg Theatre in Amsterdam (Yad Vashem.org)
where arrested Jews were registered and then sent to work details or
concentration camps (Beeldbank WO2).

our small country, bringing a deep chill to our hearts. The Jews would be either immediately exterminated or become forced labor, while living conditions were brutal. The death rates were extremely high and very few people lived through being in a concentration camp.

SS troops were always in the camps, along with the camp commander and guards, all whom would just as soon kill Jews as look at them unless they could get them to do their work. The living conditions at the concentration camps were brutal and the death rates high. If you couldn't work, you were quickly killed. If you could work, you were worked to death at hard labor in every kind of weather, with constant brutal beatings. Most of the guards were sadistic and cruel, taking sick pleasure from humiliating Jews, handing out a little bread and weak soup each day, laughing at the starving, sometimes raping the women and young girls and then kicking others out into the cold to die of exposure. Although it seems strange, lice, fleas and bedbugs were some of the Jews' friends, because if the guards thought the Jewish Rats had lice, they would not be as quick to rape the women or enter their sleeping quarters. (In "The Hiding Place" by Corrie Ten Boom, the fleas were considered a gift from God so the guards stayed out and they could have their Bible studies.) Still, the goal was degradation and then extermination by work, beatings, exposure or whatever means accomplished their goal.

Worst for all Jews were the barbaric medical experiments by doctors, especially Dr. Josef Mengele, the angel of death. He would do horrific experiments on children and women, on the genitals of men and on people's brains. They would measure brains to see if anyone had brains like people in Tibet who they thought were early forefathers of Aryans. There was evidence of ghastly experiments on children for no medical reason. One was when two boys about four years old were sewn together like Siamese twins, sharing blood veins. When they came back to the living quarters with festering wounds, gangrene and screaming in pain all night, it was more than their mothers could bear. Somehow their mothers got hold of some morphine and ended their suffering. Castrations or sterilizations were considered important experiments by the Nazis to stop the racial filth and contamination of the Jews.

Another "reason" for some of the cruel experiments was that the doctors wanted to know how German pilots who had to eject from their planes could live, so subjects were exposed to freezing temperatures, high altitudes, freezing water and other terrible scenarios to study how they reacted to difficult circumstances. After they died, which all of them typically did in diabolically horrible ways, they would be dissected to see how much air or blood was in their cranial cavity. Experiments on eyes trying to change their eye colors to Aryan blue often left the subjects blinded for several days or permanently until they died. Nazis twisted science to fit their need to discard through genocide those not suitable for the Aryan master race

*My brother Leo's false
identification card without the
"J" for Jew and professional
pose (LEFT).*

of the great German Empire.

The Jews who worked at the concentration camps did so only to buy some time so that they were not immediately exterminated and remain alive a little longer. The Nazis allowed nothing to get in the way of the annihilation of the Jews. In October, hundreds of men were sent to Austria to work in the

Jews running from the Nazis (Photograph in Public Domain).

salt mines. Most of them died there.

The German lies weren't hidden anymore. The light of truth showed the Nazis for the brutes they were and the Jews knew that deportation meant death. Jews had to report and get a permit if they moved or were traveling. The Nazis wanted to know where we were so they could gather us up and send us to the camps. In late 1941, a deportation plan was put into action that removed all of the Jews from all the provinces and concentrated them in Amsterdam. This phase was launched on 14 January 1942, beginning with the town of Zaandam. The Dutch nationals among the Jews were ordered to move to Amsterdam, while those who were from other countries were sent to Westerbork, a transit camp near Drenthe that was built and maintained by the proceeds from confiscated property of Jews.

My father brought back a Westerbork Concentration Camp

Jews in Amsterdam at assembly point prior to their deportation (holocaustresearchproject.org) and Jews waiting for train to take them to death camps (United States Holocaust Memorial Museum).

bill worth 50 cents. He was arrested and held in Westerbork in 1944 and finally liberated by the British in 1945. Although many concentration camps had money (scrip), it had absolutely no value outside of the camp. This would make sure that if people escaped, they would not have any money to spend.

We heard stories of some artistic happenings in some transit places or ghettos, but we didn't give much credence to them. Yes, we heard about a play or an opera, but we just thought it was more lies by the Germans. We did know that although some things were forbidden, some ghetto areas got by with secrets, including smuggling, marriages and quietly "celebrating" holidays. This year my 15th birthday was quietly celebrated. My mother had bartered for a part of a candy bar for me and my father had obtained a little cake through the Black Market – our family, including my grandparents of course, shared the cake. We burned a candle late into the night, reminiscing about times before the War. As I look back, I would not say it was a joyous time, but compared to the next year, it should have been enjoyed more by each one of us.

Chapter Four: 1942

At the end of last year and at the beginning of this one, Jews across Holland were ordered to move to Amsterdam. It started on 17 January with the town of Zaandam, but all Jews from the provinces were ordered to relocate to certain, specific sections of Amsterdam, stuffing more and more people into smaller quarters never meant to hold so many people. And as if to show how stupid they were, the Nazis on 23 January, decreed that no Jews were allowed to drive cars anymore. There wasn't any petrol anyway. People shook their heads, trying to figure out the sense of it all, still trying to figure out the logic of something that was completely senseless. It only got worse, with more inane decrees. There's not a lot of sunshine in Holland anyway, and the drizzle and grey skies added to the depression enveloping the country.

Then came the decree that stopped many of us in our tracks. All Dutch citizens, including the Jews, had to go to where they had registered last year and be issued an Identification Card. These identification cards had to be on your person at all times and shown to any German who wanted to check them. Now that they had us cornered tighter, they had the gall to charge each of us money for our own identification papers. Without this ID card, you could not get food coupons and without coupons, you could buy no food. Then, to make things even more complicated for the Jews, they had a letter "J" for "Jew" next to their picture. My father's picture had a "J" next to his picture, but my mother's did not because she was not Jewish. My card, received when I was 15, had the "J" next to my picture, but that would change in a little more than a year when I bought my false identification papers. Now, I could get coupons, but they now knew for sure that I was a Jew and they knew exactly where I lived. This made rounding up, transporting and killing the Jews much easier for our occupying troops.

We Jews had been in Amsterdam for centuries. The Netherlands had always been a safe haven for refugees and Jewish people had spent a lot of time leaving places or getting kicked out of countries including Spain and Portugal. My great-great-grandparents were persecuted in the 1800's in Spain and immigrated to Holland and settled in the small town of Elburg. Speaking of refugees, just take a look at the Pilgrims who founded America. These Puritans passed through Holland, living for awhile in Leiden when England would not tolerate their non-conforming religious beliefs.

Amsterdam was very open-minded about Jews' settlement here, too. Of course, this beautiful city also liked to make money and the Jews have always been skilled at that. Before the War, we were the world's center for the diamond trade.

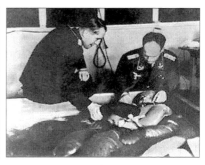

Medical experiments included lack of air (like pilots),
freezing water and cranial testing
(United States Holocaust Memorial Museum).

That disappeared during the War since that trade was mostly in the hands of Jewish businessmen and craftsmen. The diamond industry has moved to Natanya, Israel, which is another wonderful story of Jews contributing to Jews.

Centuries ago when the Protestant Church, which was the official religion of the state, wanted to rid Amsterdam of their Jews, the secular leaders weren't in any hurry to evict them. The Jews were talented merchants and traders, contributing richly to the coffers of the city, whose leaders "welcomed" these money producing Jews. Many Jews were successful in international trading of many and various commodities, including tobacco, sugar refining and printing. You need to understand that the Jewish quarter of earlier times was not a ghetto in the sense of a ghetto during the War. Before the War, this was just a neighborhood. Jews could live throughout the city and non-Jewish people could live in Jewish neighborhoods. Even the artist Rembrandt van Rijn lived on Jodenbreestraat or Jewish Broad Street in the Jewish quarter. Now, the Gestapo was changing years of positive growth and turning instead to hate and isolation.

With the War going on and on, the Germans were running short of Germans. They sent letters to all the men in Holland, demanding that they had to work for them as forced labor. The only way Germany could continue to succeed in this War was to have the labor force they needed. The only way they could get that was from the countries they occupied. I was 15 years old

LEFT: Vught death camp (Jewishgen.org).
RIGHT: Mauthausen bodies in trench. BELOW: dead bodies in wagons
(Photographs in Public Domain).

The gallows were often used to kill and intimidate prisoners (Photograph in Public Domain).

this year and received one of those letters, telling me to report to the Jewish Theater, *De Hollandsche Schouwburg Theatre*, in Amsterdam. When the letter came, I didn't know what to do but obey. My parents were stunned, too, and, unwillingly, decided they had to let me go. We walked around in a daze, gathering my belongings and going over the list again and again. The fear the Gestapo relied on worked extremely well in getting people to do what they were told to do. We knew the consequences. If you resisted you would be imprisoned or shot.

I had my duffel bag or rucksack packed with 2 pair of socks, 2 underwear, 2 blankets, 2 sets of sheets, drinking cup, fork, sweater or pullover and other necessities. I walked to the Theater. It was very hard to leave my parents and grandparents because none of us knew if we'd ever see each other again. The men and other young men there with me were picked up in army trucks and we were all transported to the small Dutch city of Alphen on the Rhine. This place was about 40 miles from Amsterdam and it was where I was to receive board and room in a Dutch civilian home.

The Germans came around early every morning and would truck us to the building sites where we would be building concrete bunkers all day along the coast. The problem, and the thing I did not really like, was getting shot at by the British

TOP: Westerbork Concentration Camp bill worth 50 Cents
BOTTOM: Westerbork String Orchestra
(United States Holocaust Memorial Museum).

planes while we worked. The British had no way to know that I wasn't there voluntarily and that I was a Dutch Jew and not a German Nazi. As far as they were concerned I was working on

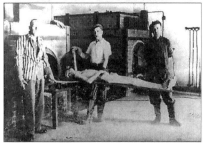

Newly liberated prisoners demonstrated how they would gather and burn bodies in the crematorium (From private pictures of American Pvt. Benjamin Oblaczynski used by permission of Debbie Book. BOTTOM LEFT: from Mauthausen Memorial Archives).

a war bunker and they didn't want it there so they didn't want me making it. It was a difficult situation and the Germans were happy to make us take all the risks since they didn't care if we got shot and died. That would save them the bother of killing us later when they had taken all the good out of us.

"Seventeen," I lied to her. Well, I was close enough and I did not want to seem like a kid to this woman. I'd been here working on the bunkers for three weeks and had definitely noticed that the daughter of my Dutch hosts, who were forced to board me, was easy on the eyes and she liked talking to me. It was the first time a woman, she was actually 17 after all, had really paid much attention to me.

We talked a lot, although you could see that her parents weren't too happy about me being there. They had a lot of other things on their minds. Both of them still worked, so they were tired when they finally got home. She was definitely a woman and there were things she was showing me that I'd never seen or felt before. Sometimes I felt so awkward that I couldn't catch my breath, let alone pretend I was knowing and worldly. This becoming a man, at fifteen, scared and excited me more than the dangers surrounding me. She was as sick of the war as everyone and liked getting away from home. We would go out at night in the village to have a beer in a small café and later, we'd sneak into the countryside or someone's stable. She didn't seem to care, even if she did know, that I wasn't really seventeen or eighteen or whatever.

Then, when I was talking to my parents one night on the phone, they informed me that the letter to work that I had received was a mistake. They told me to come back to Amsterdam because it was supposed to be for men 18 years and older. That sounded good to me so I told my boarding family of the mistake and I was sorry I had to leave. I knew I would miss the good times I had with their daughter. My girlfriend was no innocent virgin deflowered by me; more like I had been deflowered by her. She had taught me a lot and I had been more than willing to learn more. I was grateful to her for seducing me, which I should say was fun and I thanked her for that. It was an eye-opening three months for this Jewish kid from Amsterdam.

Up until now, I had never really understood the dirty talk of the men I worked with, although I laughed anyway so they'd think I did. Now, *jah,* yes, I knew what their talk was about and men I worked with could tell what I had learned. Now they accepted me in from the outer edges of manhood into the men's circle. The crass jibes and jokes, the knowing laughs and dirty gestures all locked me in with the big boys. I was sorry that I had to leave, but I was also glad to go back to Amsterdam. I worked for my uncle who was manufacturing planters from old metal cans. I helped make Christmas items by spraying white paint on them to look like snow.

Although I had changed in those three months, it was secondary to what was happening to our country. Decree after decree after decree kept coming until you could hardly stand them, robbing us Jews of all our humanity, treating us as less than animals. Jewish doctors, nurses, attorneys and all professional people were not allowed to have non-Jewish clients. And another decree: sex was forbidden between Jews and Gentiles and was punishable by law. A marriage like my parents' was no longer allowed. And yet another decree that had been set up earlier was formalized. Jews were not permitted to get married, period. That is why Leo and Jetty could not marry. The Germans didn't want Jewish families and they surely didn't want Jewish children, like little rats running around in that disgusting movie,

Germans were everywhere during the occupation (ww2incolor). Jews ready for deportation (Photograph in Public Domain).

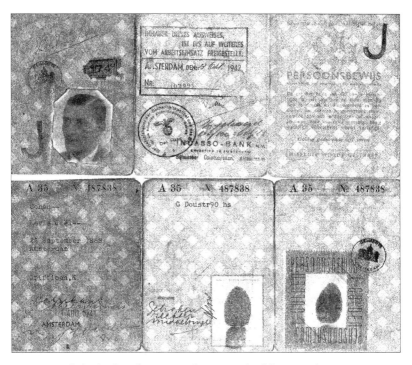

My father's identification cards. Notice the "J" next to his picture identifying him as a Jew.

"The Eternal Jew," they showed across Europe.

The next decree was serious to the Orthodox Jews in that the Germans forbade ritual slaughter of animals, which was very complicated for the religious Jews. Most of the Jewish butcher shops were forced to close and kosher meats were impossible for an ordinary Jew to obtain. The Orthodox Jews talked to their Rabbi about this problem, and the Rabbis said for them to do what they had to do to live. So now Jews even could, according to the Rabbis, eat pork if it meant survival. Everything was upside down in my world.

The next decree truly made us marked people. After the incident in the Jewish quarter in the ice cream parlor last year, the Germans came up with one of the worst decrees of all. On 29 April, Decree 13 required the mandatory wearing, by all Jews, of the Star of David, the Jewish Star. After that date, when appearing in public, Jews would have to wear this yellow Star with the Dutch word, *Jood* (Jew), on it and the badge had to be sewn over the left breast of the clothing. On outer clothing, Jews had to wear the Star on an armband.

This was mandatory for all Jews 6-years-old and older. Not wearing the Star meant being arrested and put for six months in jail, plus a 1000 guilder fine. With rationing making us very careful, we Jews even had to pay four cents and a clothing ration coupon to get the Star. With the Star on our chests, we could be spotted a mile away. We were an easy target, now, for Germans to pick us up. Of course, my family had to wear them, too, except for my mother. I remember the tears in her eyes as she sewed "*Jood*" on father's and her two children's clothes. We tried to tell her it wasn't so bad, but she knew better and the fear for us and for my father settled heavy on her heart.

My mother was a hero during the War, taking care of her family, working for the Underground, trying to hide people and help them live. Maybe it was because she had been born in a windmill (her father owned four of them), but my mother,

Kuintje (Griffioen) Cohen, was a caring and tough lady. She did not have to wear the Star so she could go about her business with a lot less harassment and without being pointed out. Her focus was on helping Jews and others who were under attack from the Nazis. She got very good at smuggling and hiding people. She will always remain my hero for all she did for those

Letter requiring Jew to report for work detail or deportation (annefrank.org/secretannex).

she loved and for those who needed her help.

There were many other Dutch Gentiles who risked much to help the Jews and we will always be grateful. The atrocities were similar across Europe. This movie shows how the horrible injustices against Jews spurred many people to work to help them. One of the finest examples of the underground Resistance, the helping of people, and faith in the midst of horror was Corrie ten Boom and her family. Read her book, "The Hiding Place," for an inside view of brave Dutch people doing the right thing in a wrong world. Many Jews were saved through her Underground network. She and her family amazingly never stopped even when the danger was very close. Even after she and her family were discovered and sent to concentration camps, she never fully gave in to despair. She knew Yahweh very well. Corrie survived, but her father, older sister and nephew died. Unfortunately, almost a third of Gentiles who helped the Dutch Jews were murdered, too. Anyone remotely connected to the "despicable ones" was targeted by the Nazis.

There were more good people who also resisted the Nazis, not only in Holland but in all the European countries suffering from the maniac Adolf Hitler. Many people stood up for others and for their own countries. Sometimes we were a little embarrassed because our Queen and family left us immediately when we were invaded. We all knew about the King of Denmark who refused to make the Jewish people of his country wear yellow Stars of David on their clothing and rode through the streets of Copenhagen every day, encouraging his people. We also knew he didn't resist much more than that and was soon only a puppet King. We all knew of good people who did good things during the War and that was often our only hope. We were in the middle of the Holocaust; yet there was a humane entity that shone through the darkness. It had to be Yawweh watching over His people even in this wickedness; we were very grateful to Him.

This was the kind of bunker I worked on at Alphen and later at Zwolle (Photograph in Public Domain).

Jah, there were many good Dutch Gentiles, helping the Jews and all those the Gestapo hated. Unfortunately, there were some not so good Dutch people, too. War is an interesting phenomenon in that it seems to either bring out the good or the bad in people. There doesn't seem to be an in-between. As I mentioned before, members of the NSB would harass the Jews, but adding to our misery was the fact that we were often defrauded by Gentile Dutch people who we thought we could trust because they were our countrymen after all.

For instance, on my father's side, there was a family, Vischraper, who owned a small department store and were quite wealthy. At that time some Jews were able to buy their way out of Holland by people taking them by train through Belgium and France and from there, through the mountains into Switzerland. This travel was illegal, but could be done if you had the connections and the money. So this group of eight people had made this arrangement and my mother and I went to their store with my tricycle to help them get their belongings to the train station early in the morning. We took all their small suitcases and went to the Central railroad station to meet the people who were supposed to take them on their flight from Holland. After three hours of waiting, it was obvious that they were bamboozled of their money. Worst of all, these people not only took their money, but also betrayed their plan to the Germans. The next day all of this family was arrested and sent to a concentration camp and never returned. Their store and home were confiscated by the Germans.

This happened to many Jewish people who were betrayed by their own countrymen as when my grandparents decided to hide all their jewelry with some Gentile friends and had me take the jewelry box to those people. I distinctly remember bringing the box to these people and talking with them about how much they wanted to help us and how horrible the Nazis treated us, for no reason at all. After the War, when my father went over to visit them and ask for the jewelry box back, they looked at him and said, "What jewelry?" They claimed that I had never brought any jewelry to them and my father realized that there was no recourse for us. All was lost. So he left their home with nothing but one more defeat and betrayal to us. Even that little bit of jewelry would have helped our family immensely after the War.

Life was confusing here in Holland when you didn't know who was on your side or who was against you. Unfortunately for many Jews and others, not all Dutch people resisted against our occupiers. Many Dutch either chose to just go along with the Germans or were forced to do so; even joining the German army in the Waffen-SS. In fact, we found out later that between 20,000 to 25,000 men voluntarily joined the Waffen-SS, fighting on the Eastern Front, in Belgium and even in our own country, the Netherlands. To our shame, several soldiers in the Nederland brigade distinguished themselves during the Battle of Narva and received the Nazi's highest award for bravery. Many companies in Holland worked for the Germans. Many of us Hollanders could not fathom such treachery. Were they blind? Didn't they see how the Germans were destroying Holland? I knew that people were working with the Nazis, but I never understood it. Those in hiding were often terrified of our own people, not knowing who would turn them in for the bounty or just because they could.

We all feared the Henneicke Column which was a group of about eighteen Hollanders who searched out and delivered hiding Jews to the Germans for about 25 guilders (about $50) each. We found out at the end of the War that this group had helped capture between 8,000 to 9,000 Jews, gave them over to the Gestapo where they were sent first to Westerbork concentration camp. They were then sent to Sobibor, Auschwitz and other concentration camps where most of them were murdered. When they ran out of people, the Column tracked hidden Jewish property. Its members were bounty hunters of the worst kind.

The Nazis wanted to murder the Jews, but they also wanted their wealth to finance their War efforts. So now, all the Jews had to hand over all their jewelry and personal art collections. However, they could keep wedding rings and pocket watches. The Germans knew they would take them from the Jews when they went to the concentration camps anyway.

Germans told the Jews they had to deposit their money in banks "for safe keeping." From the money that they had to deposit into special bank accounts, a family could only draw 250 guilders a month. Later, even that was confiscated and Jews were not allowed to even own a bank account. But now, when you had a bank account, the Nazis knew you had money and would wait at the banks and grab you, deporting you and then seizing all your money. Many very rich Jews were taken in this manner. Banks were very dangerous places for Jews. My family and others hid whatever we could and only handed over a token amount of money and jewelry. The rest we carefully hid.

The Germans were taking our valuables, our property, our money and our lives. They wanted to be done with the ghettos and with us. Himmler and Eichmann had honed the evacuations of the ghettos with the running of trains from ghettos to transit camps or concentration camps. Now, the Germans were straining to be finished with the ghettos. This year, with the implementation of the "Final Solution," our occupiers began destroying all the ghettos as the Jews and other minorities were quickly deported immediately either to forced-labor or concentration camps, bypassing the ghettos. Nazis hoped to have most of the Jews annihilated by the end of next year. If their wish came true, my father, brother and me would be dead

LEFT: Eternal Jew poster (WW2shots) and BELOW: Orthodox Jews (Photograph in Public Domain).

very soon. That pressure is what all Jews lived under every minute or everyday.

The Seyss-Inquart's decrees kept coming, following other decrees until we were exhausted by the stupidity and absurdity of it all. One decree was that Jews may not fish may by making it

*Kosher butcher in Windsheim displaced persons camp and Jewish
butcher shop in Amsterdam
(United States Holocaust Memorial Museum).*

*Star of David patch (Photograph in Public Domain)
and armbands sold by emaciated woman
(United States Holocaust Memorial Museum) Roll of yellow Star of
David fabric (Jewish Historical Museum Amsterdam) .*

illegal for us to obtain a fishing license. We were not dismissive
of this decree because many Jews were being forced to starve
to death. Also, Jews were not allowed to play organized sports.

99

We had never been so regulated by such petty details. We were in a constant state of perpetual state of fear because we may have made some infraction of some decree that we didn't know existed. It was almost impossible to know all of them and which made us susceptible to imprisonment and transferred to a concentration camp.

The Germans' attention was distracted somewhat from us because something Hitler never wanted to happen occurred. After Pearl Harbor last December, the United States had declared war against Germany and Japan. The Germans got more serious about fortifying Holland's coast as they evacuated resorts and villages on the coast and intensified work on Holland's part of the Atlantic Wall. This wall was the "most ambitious military fortification program of World War II" and stretched over 5,000 kilometers along the Atlantic coastline, from the Spanish border to the Arctic Circle.

Now that the United States had entered the war, the Germans were sure that there would be some sort of British and United States landing along the Atlantic coast and they were on alert. The German leader, Von Rundstedt, was working on a defensive/offensive where troops would be immediately sent to the sites once the invasion happened. Holland had excellent roads which made this tactic possible. Germans were fortifying this wall with huge cement bunkers (some I worked on) with turreted naval guns in Belgium and the Netherlands. This was the first-line Flak (from the German word *Flugzeugabwehrkanone*) aircraft defense cannons and they needed more workers. The Germans pushed their enlistment of Dutch men to do the labor. If a man resisted, he was imprisoned and then shot. Many people who were forced to work on German projects demonstrated their passive resistance by working slowly and ineffectively.

It was expensive to develop and build those behemoth guns and the Germans always needed more money. They were trying to get it in many different ways so it was not such a shock one evening when we were visited by four Germans. The door bell rang, and because I was the youngest kid in the house, I was the one who had to see who was at the door. After I opened it, I was standing there totally speechless. In front of me were four Germans: a German SS Officer in black uniform, a sailor, a German police officer and a woman. They asked me where my father was and said that they were authorized to conduct a search for Black Market items. I was very afraid and thought that we were all doomed.

They barged their way into our house and went all over the place, searching all rooms and turning things over. Since my father was heavily involved in black marketing, they had a hay day and found 50 pounds of tobacco, bags of dried green beans, a large amount of rice, rolls of materials and other illegal things. As they were loading all of this in a large German army truck, all of us, my father, Leo, Jetty, my mother and me were standing in the living room with a couple of pistols pointed at us. That's when I looked at the woman and said to her in German, *"Wir*

Oskar Schindler and some of the people he helped save (United States Holocaust Memorial Museum) and Corrie Ten Boom in front of the tiny hiding place crafted into her upstairs bedroom (Corrie Ten Boom Museum).

erhkuhnen unze" (I recognize you). I remembered her from Alphen on the Rhine, the little Dutch city where the Germans had sent me to work between Utrecht and Leiden.

What happened is that when I was with the girl in Alphen, we would go out and have a beer in this small café and I remembered seeing this woman there. After I made that remark, she did not respond to me, but started to talk in German to the officer in the black uniform. Right after she talked to him, he gave my father a piece of paper and told him to present himself the next day at this German police headquarters. After giving my father this piece of paper, they all left.

Something wasn't right. My father started to call some friends and told them about what happened. One of his friends, a jewelry store owner, had experienced the same thing, but had kept quiet about it. Much later we learned of a gang of thieves that would target typical Jewish named business people and then would rob them. They knew that the Jews were probably dealing in the black market items and were less likely to report it to report it to the Germans.

Some weeks later, I was riding my bicycle downtown and all of a sudden, I see this same SS officer in black uniform with two girls on his arms. He's walking with them towards the Kalverstraat, which is a famous street in downtown Amsterdam, with all kinds of entertainment shops, bars and movie theaters. After I saw them, I parked my bicycle and went to a phonebooth and, all excited, called my father and told him that I had seen the officer. Before he could say anything, I told my father that I was going to follow them and hung up so my father couldn't tell me not to do it. Even then, we knew forgiveness was easier to receive than permission.

Now, you have to realize that I was a brazen, stupid kid and never should have done what I did. I started to follow them and after a little while, I think he felt that he was being followed and he looked back a couple of times. In the meanwhile, I was trying to figure out what to do. Finally on the dam square, where the Royal Palace is, I saw a policeman and tried to explain to him what was going on, but he could not leave his post to help me. So, I continued to follow them until something maybe would come up.

Finally, I got lucky. The officer and his girlfriends decided that they would take in a movie, so they purchased tickets and went inside the theater. I knew that they would be occupied for at least one and a half hours and so I went to a large police station a few blocks away. I found a few German police officers who listened to me as I told them what had happened at our house and about the people in the movie theater who had stolen our property. They believed what I told them and followed me to the theater where they went inside with a flashlight and picked them out in the dark and arrested him with his two female friends.

I was afraid for the first time of what I had done. Here was a Jewish kid with a Jewish Star on his chest accusing this German officer of a crime. The German police came around with a couple of police cars and put the two girls in one car and me with the officer in the back of the other car. As I was sitting next to him, he said to me, "You will be shot for this, for having a German officer arrested." So I answered him that I did not care. It was a long ride to the police station.

Upon arrival at the Gestapo headquarters, they asked me where my father was and I told them he was at home. They asked me where I lived and sent out a car to pick him up. They brought him in after a little while and he took the chair next to me. I could tell that my father was worried because all the things that this man and his gang had stolen were illegal Black Market items which we were not supposed to possess and now he had to tell the Germans. I was really worried. To get myself into trouble was one thing, but to involve my father was terrible. I feared what they would do to him and berated myself for my stupidity. We were waiting for at least three hours, when all of a sudden, a high ranking German officer came up to us and told me to stand up. As I did so, he started to shake my hand and complimented me in German for what I had done. I was speechless and deeply surprised.

As it turned out, the German police searched this SS officer and found an address book on him with 16 names and addresses and arrested all of his cohorts within the hour, while we were there waiting. We wondered if they had been trying to catch this man for sometime because they seemed to know a lot about what the group of thieves had done.

After they went to court, out of the 16 arrests, four of them were executed. The reason for that was that the SS officer in black had stolen the uniform from his brother who died on the Russian front and wasn't even an officer or even a soldier. The sailor and German policeman and another officer were executed for war crimes. The others were sent to concentration camps and some of them that came back were prosecuted by the Dutch government after the War. I still have the newspaper clipping my father sent to me in Indonesia; where I was after the War.

A few weeks later my father received a phone call from the police headquarters to come to pick up the merchandise that was stolen from us. When Father went there, you could not believe how polite they were. Here, they were returning Black Market items that we, as Jews, were not even supposed to have. Despite all of our justified fears, we were stunned by the actions of the German police officers returning our items and treating us as humans when returning our item. We were after all their enemies because we were Jews.

After we received our returned items, we became more

cautious than ever before. We we were no longer hidden; in fact, we were known. The Germans knew who we were, what we had and where we lived. From that moment on, we were always on high-alert and on the lookout which contributed to our constant anxiety.

As much as we paid attention to what was going on with the decrees, Germans and the Allies, life started to return back to "normal" or as normal as it could be considering what was happening daily. We went on in our personal lives to the best of our ability.

These pictures show what the Nazis considered successful in reaching their "Final Solution," the extermination of all Jews (Photographs in Public Domain).

Wagon loads of dead bodies at Buchenwald (United States Holocaust Memorial Museum).

My mother and I were secretly taking care of 12 Jewish people who were hiding on the 3rd floor and attic of a nearby house. There were many others in similar situations that were forced into hiding, starving and living in fear from the terror of the SS. Of the 12 Jews we were helping, each of them had received their letter, demanding they get ready for resettlement and each knew exactly what that meant. My mother and I would go to their homes and bring them things in my old wagon to their hiding spots. We would bring groceries, clothing and other items that they needed or asked of us. This was quite difficult because we had to buy everything on the Black Market because these people had no ration coupons as they were in hiding.

These wonderful people included my Aunt Sophia Andriesse Cohen, my cousin Mizzi (who was a well-known ballet dancer) and my cousin, Jacques, who had been named after me. It was sad to see how they changed while they lived there for all those many months. My cousin, Mizzi, who was a ballerina prior to the War, looked like a very malnourished young girl because she had been inside all the time, unable to see the sun and was starving. One day on our normal visit to the hiding house, my mother and I encountered a serious problem. One of the men of the group that we had been helping had died. We had to get his body out from the third floor without anyone suspecting that others were hiding in this building. We waited until that evening since we had to do it by ourselves because no one else could be seen. My mother and I wrapped the dead man in newspapers and dragged his body down three flights of steep stairs, each only about 6" deep. We carried/dragged him three blocks down the street to a city park where we left him to be found by the police.

My mother and I took care of these people for many months, struggling to be unseen and unknown. The terribly sad part of this story is that later when I was hiding out myself, the group was betrayed by a woman from who they bought fish every week. She received 25 guilders per person for her betrayal. They were all arrested, plus the man they rented the floor from. All of them sent to Auschwitz. The only one who survived was the man who rented the floor to them, Mr. Ver Gelder. The rest were all murdered at Auschwitz. It bothered my family so much that they were sold out by a fellow Dutch citizen, not a German spy or soldier. This taught me not to trust anyone and I

ABOVE: German bunkers along the coast (Photographs in Public Domain).

never could understand the atrocities of others for money.

My mother will always be my hero. She hid my father, Jetty, Leo, me and many more people than the group that was betrayed. She was not Jewish so she could go about her business without being harassed by the Nazis. During the War, my mother worked tirelessly to protect, hide and help many Jews and non-Jews to survive. Her efforts we the difference between life and death of so many people beyond our family. She gave so much and asked for nothing in return. Had the Germans found out what my mother had done, she would have been executed on the spot. As you'll notice in the Prologue to my book, I've dedicated this book to her. Her acts of heroism spurred me on and helped me survive. She never gave up and I've tried to emulate her in my life. I am grateful I have had my life to live. I didn't die in the War and I refused to let it kill my future. Living my life well was part of my defiance against the Nazis.

As hard as this War was on everyone, it was a terribly difficult time especially for the older Jews and the younger children. My grandparents were aware of what was going on, aware that they would probably be called out to "resettle." They really thought that was what would happen or at least they pretended they thought so. They got themselves two large trunks which they filled with their necessities, because they believed that they would get to be resettled in Theresienstadt, Poland. My father could not convince them that they could not take those big trunks because those two trunks represented all they had left after all their years of living, except for family, of course. At the time my grandmother was 78-years-old and my grandfather was 84-years-old. We had asked them if they wanted to hide time and again, but they refused. They were set in their ways. There were believers that relocation stories were true and the start of a new life was possible. I always had a suspicion that my grandparents felt that it was too much to ask of their family to hide them and that they knew the risks we were already taking and would be taking hiding or helping get them out of the country.

One night I was visiting a friend, and my parents called on the phone to tell me to come home right away. I rode home on my bicycle as fast as I could and when I walked into the house, everybody was in tears. The inevitable had arrived. The Germans had come on a raid with a large truck, already partially full with other old Jewish people, to pick up my grandparents. Of course, Oma and Opa could not take the trunks and could only take a pair of small suitcases, Opa's prayer shawl and a couple of his religious books and his *Tefillin* (two small, black leather, cube-shaped cases containing Torah texts written on parchment, which are to be worn by male Jews of 13 years and older as reminders of God and of the obligation to keep the Law during daily life).

Whenever I think about what happened next or when I am asked about what happened to my grandparents, I cannot help but cry.

The German officer told my father that my grandparents would be first taken to a nearby school that occupied by the Germans about a half mile away. I rode my bicycle, hopped off and went running toward the door. I had to see them once more. I had so much I wanted to tell them about how much I loved them. There I was met by a German guard. I asked him if I could please see my grandparents, but he was not allowed to let me do so. But he was not unfriendly and since the doors were open, he said I could look inside.

As I leaned against the doorpost and looked inside this school building crowded with old people, there were my be-loved Oma and Opa sitting on the side, together on a bench. As I told you before, that they always would bicker a little, but here they were sitting so peacefully, holding hands. As I stood there looking at my grandparents from so far away, this picture of them was to be engraved in my memory forever. This image is as clear to me today as it was when I was at looking at them that night. It has barely dimmed for me after all these years later. It was one of the saddest days of my life and made the Holocaust personal in a way I can barely express let alone handle. I stayed, watching them as long as the guard allowed me. I had hoped they would see me there, but that was not to be. After the door was closed, I still stayed there for a long time. I knew that I would never forget this moment in time and my love for my grandparents would never fade just like the image in my mind's eye.

The next day, Oma and Opa were sent to the transit camp of Westerbork (where my father was sent later in the War). After a week, they and the others boarded a railway cattle car and were shipped to the concentration camp of Auschwitz, where all older people were exterminated on arrival. My 78-year-old Oma and my 84-year-old Opa were stripped of all their belongings, sat down, fed dinner and then told to take a shower to get

By this time of the War, many bicycles no longer had rubber tires and we rode on the rims or wooden tires (Photograph in Public Domain and Dutch National Military Museum).

rid of their lice. This is when the SS gassed them exterminating my grandparents and so many others. Their deaths have always haunted me. I feel the pain of the loss now as I did then as a kid. The pain has not lessened through the years, even through we feared that this was something that would happen to them. Oma and Opa were such formative figures and full of so much love tied to my childhood and they were taken by the SS and Auschwitz. Throughout my life I have continued to miss them deeply and remember my last images of them.

Death camps often unloaded Jews from the train cars and directly led them to firing squads or gas chambers. At the camps, women and small girls were herded to one side and men and boys to the other side. All had to completely undress and the Germans would select who was physically fit for forced labor. Those Jews "chosen" to work had numbers tattooed on the inside of their arms. After that, the guards would shave everybody's hair to become blankets and socks for U-Boat captains and crew.

All of the other people who were not "chosen" to work themselves to death were told that they would have a shower. First, people were forced to remove all of their clothing and any jewelry they still had (like wedding bands) and then they were herded naked into the death chamber itself for a "shower." Once in the large shower room, they had to sit on benches. Mothers with children were told to stay together. At this point, the Germans would open a hatch on the roof of the building and drop the gas pellets that would kill the prisoners. Prisoners at the camps could hear the cries, screaming and the clawing at the walls of those trying to escape the burning, toxic fumes. There was no escape and there was no way out. Gas chambers were the efficient extermination method that Hitler had wanted and by this time Auschwitz had been expanded to have an additional gassing chamber and more crematoriums.

Birkenau, the largest death camp, gassed over 4,000 people at one time.

The Germans Hydrogen Cyanide in the form of Zyklon B gas. This gas in lower doses was used to kill lice. Too soon it was discovered by an SS officer that higher doses of the Zyklon B gas would do the work of a firing line in about 30 minutes killing everyone in the "shower". This discovery made it so that the SS no longer had to do firing squads or put a bullet in each Jew. After the air had cleared, the Jews and other prisoners who weren't gassed worked to keep the Nazi killing machine in working order. After the gas killed the prisoners, Jewish workers removed any other valuables such as gold teeth, missed rings or any remaining precious items found on the bodies.

The prisoners brought the bodies to the ovens at the crematoriums, but there were too many bodies so other solutions were implemented. The guards instructed the prisoners to dig deep ditches outside and burn the murdered Jews in the ditches. Prisoners and people outside of Auschwitz-Birkenau and other death camps could see billowing clouds of smoke in the nearby skies. Auschwitz-Birkenau was one of the most famous death camps for this type of extermination and it was where many of my relatives and friends were murdered.

My Opa and Oma were gone and I thought of them so many times throughout the day. It was incredibly difficult for anyone in my family to get over the loss of my grandparents. It was especially difficult for my father. He had become quiet and preferred more time alone. His anger would erupt at times, but we understood it was his way to cope with the grief and loss of his parents. The frustration he felt as their son and that he could not protect his own parents' genocide. Leo and Jetty respected what Father was going through, but it was also very hard on Leo and me. Our Opa had always been so very special to both of us in different ways. Mother kept on through it all. She watched over the day to day activities and pulled me back into helping her with our responsibilities to those still in hiding. Our family had reached a turning point and instead of breaking us, it encouraged us more. We would not let the Nazis kill us. But, too soon, that almost happened to my father, brother and myself.

As we tried to get back into the even more abnormal normality called life, the Germans made that more impossible. To heap more upon the Dutch Jews, now, we were not allowed

German soldiers checking IDs (Markt 12 - Euregional Hiding Museum and Photograph in Public Domain).

to ride on the street cars anymore. The tram drivers made it very clear for anyone who was a Jew never to even attempt getting on because they would throw you off. There was also a section on the car just for Germans only, not Dutch. Their noose around us kept getting tighter. By the end of June, we were not allowed out past a curfew of 8:00 in the evening until 6:00 in the morning. The times had started out at 11:00

and kept getting pushed earlier and earlier over the past few months. We had to be in our own homes. If we didn't obey, we would be arrested. Those decrees were followed by others. Jews couldn't visit non-Jews, Jewish women could not get their hair styled in a beauty salon! Beyond the insanity of the decrees, the Germans were doing everything to take away our way of life in addition to our lives.

We were only half way through the year, but now July signaled an increase in the amount of deportations to extermination camps in occupied Poland. Many went to Auschwitz, but their was also Sobibor. Sobibior was known as an extermination camp that no one ever returned from.

For the Dutch, we discovered that our police, railway workers and our friends were working with the Germans to ensure that these "cattle car" trains were full of Jews. German Nazis and Dutch Nationaal-Socialistische Beweging (NSB) members would randomly pickup and arrest Jews right off the streets. Once they were at the Jewish Theatre (still used for this), they were herded on trains and sent to Westerbork and from there, sent on to Polish concentration camps to be merged with the thousands of other Jews from other occupied countries. Another decree was that no Jews were allowed to search or occupy empty houses and apartments. If anyone was caught, you were shot or sent away to a concentration camp to be gassed. The NSB became very active in enforcing this decree. Every move was a deliberate step towards total Jewish annihilation.

Dutch NSB when the Germans occupied Holland became active enforcers and joined the movement of being anti-Jewish. Prior to the Germans occupation they were not known as being anti-Jewish. We knew this firsthand because, prior to the War, we were living in a different neighborhood and on the floor above us were some Dutch people who belonged to the NSB party, but they were not in any way anti-Jewish. This hate for our people only came about after the Germans occupation of Holland. The hatred of Jews increased as the NSB's power increased. We very close friends with this family, especially my brother, Leo, with their son. This relationship proved to be more powerful than politics and saved Leo's life later on.

The Nazis were getting fanatical about stepping up their deportations of Jews. Higher ups were again upset that Jewish extermination wasn't going faster. Some Jews were sent to labor camps, others to concentration/transit camps and still others straight to death camps. All Germans now knew exactly what the "Final Solution" was – total elimination of all Jews through extermination as rapid as possible. At every camp, starvation, disease and brutal physical abuse marked the lives of every prisoner before they were killed or died. Men's arms would be tied behind them, a hook would grab the rope at their wrists and pull the prisoners up against the wall. Screams tore through the camps as the excruciating pain of having their shoulders and arm sockets ripped out often caused men to pass out before they were let down and beaten for being weak. The Nazis had many methods to torture their captives. The gallows were still considered an effective tool and was often used to keep inmates intimidate to cooperate. Fear permeated everything in the camps. No matter what, the full extermination of the Jews was imperative for the glory of the German Aryan race and the German Empire, but brutality before that end kept the troops' morale up.

Those of us still "free" and outside the concentration camps were always on alert for the sporadic *razzias* (raids). The Nazis would swoop into a neighborhood, go door-to-door with their machine guns, hauling out whole families and putting them into trucks. The SS had high deportation quotas to meet from

German High Command and the raids increased to reach those numbers.

Allies reaching farther into German occupied territory, Hitler did not want his massacres stopped. He ordered more deaths, the cremation and burning of more bodies.

On command, the Germans started to conduct raids all over the city because they had orders that they needed forced labor for the War. Manufacturing and building demanded at least 4,000 Jews to be shipped each week. My brother, who was delivering something for my father, was trapped in the middle of such a raid and arrested. As he was forced to sit on the ground with his hands in the air. A young SS officer in a black Gestapo uniform came over to him, looked down, and said to my brother, "Leo, what the hell are you doing here?" As it turned out to be, it was his friend who had lived above us in the apartments from the family that was a member of the

TOP LEFT: Water pipes in Mauthausen gas chamber (furtherglory.wordpress.com).
TOP RIGHT: Death cell (Photograph in Public Domain).
LEFT: Scratches on wall at Auschwitz and death cell (Photograph in Public Domain).

NSB party. Leo's friend he had joined the German army, in a special Dutch SS regiment. My brother explained to him that they got him in this raid and he said to Leo, "I will yell at you and I want you to do what I tell you." So he kicked Leo around and yelled at him to get up and he pulled out his pistol and put it in Leo's back and said to him, "Walk!" So Leo started to walk and his friend took him towards the guards and told them that Leo was a special prisoner and he was taking care of him. He then walked Leo for a couple of blocks down the street and said to him, "Now get the hell out of here and good luck!" That was the last time any of our family ever saw that young man. He disobeyed his orders, risked his life to save Leo and we wanted to thank him for his kindness in saving Leo.

Leo suffered a mental breakdown. We strongly believe that it had to do with the stress of this event and the overall stresses of the War. Leo kept feeling that he was being followed and would have to find my parents and know where they were at all times. It may have been the culmination of almost meeting the same fate as Opa and Oma, feeling the gun against his neck and realizing what happened to the other Jews caught in the raid that overcame him. After the War, his paranoia improved somewhat. He and Jetty got married and had two children. His daughter Lien, son Loekie and Jetty, his faithful wife are still alive in 2014. Leo tried to work in my father's factory which Father started up again after the War. He stopped after a little while because his mind couldn't was not functioning properly anymore. He stopped playing the piano altogether.

After a short time, Leo was declared unfit to work and received some financial support from the Dutch government the rest of his life until he died. His wife, Jetty, took care of him all those years and is, in my opinion, one of the finest women I ever met, and I love her.

For many people like Leo, when the War ended, it did not

Pile of Orthodox Jews' prayer shawls found at Auschwitz after liberation (United States Holocaust Memorial Museum). One of them probably belonged to my beloved Opa who was once a young man like me (see picture of him). This picture where the German officers are cutting the hair of an Orthodox Jew is what I imagined happened to my dear Opa (Photograph in Public Domain).

end for them. The mental stresses, anxieties and stresses of being a survivor was too much for many; including Leo.

Many people committed suicide months and even years later because their torment was too much to cope with. In many cases, the Nazis succeeded in their goal to exterminate Jews.

September came and so did new decrees from the Germans. The latest was that no Jewish students could attend any college or university. All Jewish teachers and students had long ago been kicked out of public elementary and high schools. There had not been Jewish teachers in colleges or universities for over a year. All these displaced college-aged young people were smart and many became active in speaking out and publishing underground papers against the Nazis. Since they couldn't go to college, many joined the Resistance. The Nazis didn't realize how many of the college-age Jewish students went into hiding and joined the Resistance because of this one decree. If someone was found out to be part of the Resistance they would face the same fate of the Jews even if they were not Jewish.

The Germans' attempt to make Holland *Judenrein* (clean of Jews) went countrywide on 2 October. Thousands of Jews were deported from Holland this year and by November the SS hardly bothered with transit camps like Westerbork. They sent Jews straight to extermination camps like Sobibor and Auschwitz. Most Holocaust survivors hid far from German troops and moved throughout the country on forged identification documents. This is what I did the next year.

Germans lowered their age limits and started shipping younger teenagers to Germany to work in the factories. Leo was debilitated and he, with my father and I, were in hiding. I was young and healthy, so I knew I could be grabbed at anytime. The Germans knew we were Jews and they knew where we lived. I would have to learn how to be better at hiding underground. It was not easy for anyone trying to escape the Gestapo in Holland. Our own geography made it very difficult if not nearly impossible because our land was so flat. The surrounding countries along our borders were occupied by Germany or was Germany. The Western and Northern provinces

Amsterdam trams and Bus trams would not let Jews ride
(Photographs in Public Domain).

were bordered by the North Sea which was patrolled by the Germans. It was very dangerous for anyone trying to cross to the British Isles. Many died trying.

The most famous example of hiding from the Germans in Holland was the Frank family, who survived for several years hidden in an Amsterdam building not too far from my home. I did not know them. The diary kept by Anne Frank has become the most widely-read account of "life" in the *achterhuis* (back house) while her family hid from the Nazis. Her father, Otto Frank, was the only member of the Frank family that survived the Holocaust. Otto had been returned Anne's diary and he published it. Otto had been in New York in the United States of America, where he went to school as an engineer and worked at Macy's. He had moved back to Germany to take care of his ailing parents. There he married and had two beautiful daughters, Margot and Anne. Margot also wrote her diary, but it was never found.

Take Anne Frank's account from her diary and multiply it by tens of thousands and you will have a sample of what the Nazis did to the Jews and others Hitler deemed worthy of annihilation in the Netherlands and other European countries. You will have a sense of the fear and the unnecessary evil of it all. There was so much suffering during the War that nothing can truly portray the horror upon horrors so many of us endured. Over 6 Millions Jews were exterminated in diabolical ways not to mention the millions of others that were not Jewish that Hitler sentenced to be destroyed off the face of earth.

A compelling memorial that has touched me is titled "Shoes on the Danube Bank" in Budapest, Hungary. It was created by Can Togay and Gyula Pauer and is composed of 60 iron pairs of shoes permanently connected to the bank. These rusting shoes are in remembrance of the Jews who were rounded up from the nearby ghetto by the ruling Arrow Cross Party for Jewish activities. The scattered shoes are different styles and sizes depicting men, women and children and different careers. The Arrow Cross terror would force these Jews to strip naked and leave their valuable shoes on the banks. They were then commanded to face the river and a firing squad shot the prisoners in their backs so they fell into the Danube River and were washed away, causing the river to run red. This became a commonplace tragedy during 1944-1945. Then there is the picture of a warehouse overflowing with prisoners' shoes at Majdanek concentration camp in Poland around the same time.

The fact that people's shoes were deemed more valuable than human life, your understanding unforgiveable hatred must never be allowed to reign again. We must protect ourselves, each other and all humanity.

Chapter Five: 1943

The Nazis were past edgy and nasty about reaching their exterminations goals for the "Final Solution." Since the United States had entered the War, they felt the pressure to finish their mission without interruption. They really had wanted all Jews extinct by the end of last year. This January, they had carted off all the patients of the Jewish Mental Hospital and stuck them on a train to Auschwitz. The unwitting patients were quickly gassed and cremated.

January did perk us up with a bit of good news. Those of us who listened illegally to Dutch Oranje Radio were given a bright spot when Princess Margriet Francisca of the Netherlands was born in Ottawa, Ontario, Canada, to Queen Juliana and Prince Bernhard. The Nazi occupation had force the Dutch Royal family into exile in Canada since June 1940. This welcoming of good news helped cement the Netherlands' bond with Canada.

For the Dutch still living in occupied Netherlands, Margriet's birth was a message to all of us, encouraging us to stand strong

Concentration camp prisoners and open mass graves at concentration camp (Photographs in Public Domain).

and resist the wicked invaders. Margriet was named after the marguerite, a flower worn in Holland as a symbol of resistance. We knew our Queen would someday return and Holland would be "normal" again. We clung to that hope.

Our Queen wrote something about Holland being a nation of heroes, but that was political. We loved hearing stories about the Resistance and Underground, but we were also fearful because there would always be brutal repercussions, even for the Queen's messages. In February at The Hague, members of a Dutch Resistance cell shot General-Lieutenant Hendrik Seyffardt who was in charge of campaigning to get volunteer Dutch recruits for the Waffen-SS. They rang his doorbell and when he came to the door, they shot him twice and he died the next day. As could be expected, there was quick and harsh retribution. SS General Hanns Rauter ordered 50 Dutch hostages shot and killed.

One evening, I was buying some imitation cookies (they could be made from almost anything, including tulip bulbs) from a street vendor who was a friend of my mother's. I wasn't sure what these were made from, but they surely weren't the same as my Opa had once made for Leo and me. This man was

Westerbork Jews boarding deportation train (yadvashem.org). Nazis supervise loading Jews onto train headed to death camps (Photograph in Public Domain).

involved with mother in helping the Jews who were hiding. He said to me to tell my mother that a trainload of German soldiers were on their way to conduct a major raid in Amsterdam the next day and that they were in an ugly mood because they had been drinking. I quickly went home and warned my mother. We made some extra preparations and deliveries so we would not have to be out the next day.

Sure enough, the next morning, sirens went off all over the place very near our block. The raid started with the Germans blocking the street bridges, which stopped all traffic. By doing so, they were able to contain everybody from moving around. After that, they started to go street by street, into every house and looked for Jews. At that point, my father, Leo, Jetty and I were ready with our duffel bags to go – we were sure we would be arrested. They were so close and we had nowhere to hide.

While we were standing outside on the street watching what was happening on our block, the Germans on each end of the street set up machine guns which they would assuredly use if someone tried to flee. We watched them going up the stairs of one of my father's friend's house. Mr. Breem. Breem was a violin player in the Amsterdam Philharmonic Orchestra.

They brought him downstairs and took him away, never to return. We watched them grab our neighbors and we were just standing there, waiting for the worst to happen to us, expecting to get picked up and sent away, too. I felt so much fear and helplessness that I was frozen, unable to plot our escape. Suddenly, whistles all over the place were blowing and the German soldiers started to pack up their machine guns into the trucks. It was precisely 5 o'clock and their work day was over! It was time to stop their daily activity. We could not believe our good fortune in that we escaped because their work day was over. For once, the Germans' fanatical precision gave us

Auschwitz and Sobibor extermination camps in Poland
(Photograph in Public Domain and The HistoryBunker.co.uk).

Concentration camp
and prisoners
(Photographs in Public Domain).

LEFT: Jews arrested in Amsterdam - much like my brother, Leo (United States Holocaust Memorial Museum).
RIGHT: Often Jews were shot (posed Photograph in Public Domain).

our lives back, if only for the time being. It was a reminder for us not to allow ourselves to be that vulnerable and immobile again.

Shortly after this experience, my letter came again and again demanding that I report on such and such a date to the Jewish Theatre to be deported to Germany to work there. We had a family counsel about this and everyone decided I would not be as fortunate this time as I had been last time. It was decided

I would need to leave my home and hide out for the rest of the War as thousands of others had been doing. I was now 16-years-old and had received THE letter calling me up to go and register for forced labor in Germany. There was no waiting until I was 18. We were smarter than the first time they called me up. It was decided that I could not afford to take a chance that I would live through another German capture, especially with Germany in hand-to-hand-combat with the Soviets. I would have to go into hiding only I didn't know anywhere to go or who to hide with. It would be too dangerous to hide out with the others my mother and I had been taking care of for all this time. We talked about different towns and cities, different areas of Holland that might be less dangerous and even places we had visited or vacationed as possibilities for me to go into hiding. Lucky for Leo, he didn't get a letter. My mother hid father, Leo and Jetty for the rest of the War,

I had saved up some money, so I got myself and Leo some new ID papers without the "J" in case he needed to hide later on. Without the J on our identification papers, Leo and I were not marked as Jews. I started to look for a place to go underground. There were many places to get forged papers, but I had to be sure to get the very best I could afford if we wanted to fool the Germans. The Germans would take my life in an instant if they even suspected it was a fake. I packed a duffel bag with just a few things and packed my mind with a lot of precious memories. I knew that I may never see any of my family again. During the lonely times, I would take those memories out and relish them, even smells and tastes, only to have them close and disappear back into the recesses of my mind as terror of reality forced them away. I was Jewish, and Jews were taught never to give up hope or faith.

Our small country, packed with over 9 million people, was not geographically favored with forests or mountains, so there weren't very many places to hide except in homes or on farms or in some type of buildings. If I had not gone into hiding, it was almost assured that I would be deported to a work camp or to Auschwitz or to the death camp of Sobibor. Out of 60,000 Jews who were deported to Auschwitz, less than 1,000 survived the War. Out of 34,000 Jews who were deported to Sobibor, only two (2) people lived and returned to the Netherlands! Some Jews actually escaped from Sobibor. Of the almost 100,000 Jews who did not go into hiding, only about 1,000 survived the War. I wanted to survive and so I did what I had to do. I prepared to leave my family for an unknown future of hiding for my life. I had to learn how to hide very quickly and to do it carefully or I'd end up dead. The rest of the family decided that from there on, my father, Leo and Jetty would stay hidden in the house and would not go outside the house anymore during the daytime. The only person to go out would be my mother who could freely go around and take care of things. Because that last raid was in our neighborhood, it would be pretty well safe for a few weeks anyway. I would make sure I had everything I needed and I put out feelers about places available to hide.

The year marched on. In April, all the Jews found in the province of Noord Brabant were ordered to report to camp Vught for their next orders. It was a death bell for all of those people and they knew it. Fear was our constant emotion, though I would try to push it down. More and more Jews were forced to go into hiding and it was getting a little crowded in the underground. It was going to get worse and more difficult. In May, Heinrich Himmler declared that most Jews had to be deported or report for work by the end of the year. The rate of deportations was accelerated again as the Germans continued to erase us Jews off the face of the earth.

The authorities ordered 7,000 Jews, including employees of the Jewish council in Amsterdam who had been the liaison

LEFT: Shoes along the Danube (Wikipedia)

BELOW: Shoes outside a filled warehouse at Majdanek concentration camp in Poland (United States Holocaust Memorial Museum).

and sort of governing body of the ghetto, to assemble in an Amsterdam city square for deportation. Only 500 people actually complied with what everyone knew was a death decree. Jews were catching on and weren't so quick to make our deaths easy. This made the Germans very angry and they sealed off the Jewish quarter and rounded up Jews at any and all hours of the day. There was no rest from the Germans and woe to anyone hiding and getting caught. The Germans would make those Dutch Jews pay with their lives almost immediately, which some thought was more advantageous than waiting and waiting for death. But, if they didn't kill you they sent you to a concentration camp. Convict Jews (Jews in hiding who were caught) were punished much more severely in

Anne, Edith and Margot Frank. Anne and her sister Margot with other German Jewish refugee children playing tea time with their dolls in Amsterdam (United States Holocaust Memorial Museum).

129

Warehouses in Majdanek and Auschwitz overflowing with clothes and suitcases (United States Holocaust Memorial Museum).

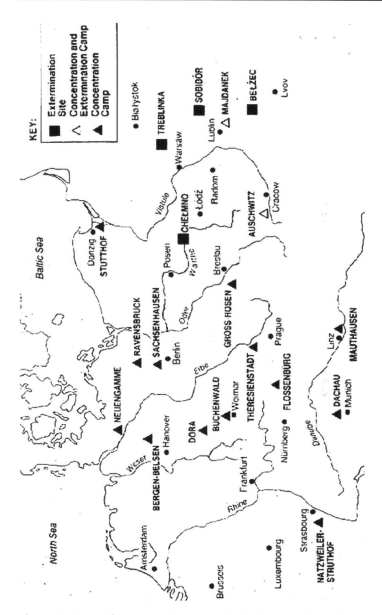

Concentration and extermination camps in Netherlands, Poland and Germany (teacheroz.com).

the concentration camps by guards. They made death seem a relief from they would face in the concentration camps.

In May and June, the Nazis intensified their *razzias* – raids of the Jews in Amsterdam. Screams, running, scuffling, sporadic shots and angry shouts were heard every day and every evening. There weren't any safe houses or places anywhere anymore. In May, there was a widespread strike in Amsterdam, Arnhem and Hilversum against the conscriptions and deportations. Artur Seyss-Inquart imposed court-martials against the strikers and a hefty fine of 18 million guilders against the businesses and individuals who were part of the strike. His iron hand stopped such uprisings immediately. He was so angry at Jews, he demanded all streets named after Jews be changed. Signs were torn down and streets were renamed and they put up more signs keeping Jews out of more places.

Half way into this year, thousands more young men were sent notices demanding they report in at the Jewish Theater to be sent to Germany for forced labor. A lot of them, too, went into hiding. Because of that, Resistance expanded and became a wide network. Unfortunately, some people joined only to betray them. The Germans were angry that more young men hadn't reported to work. They responded to the stepped up Resistance with intimidation and violence. Over the course of the War, almost 20,000 Dutch ended up in prison because of their work in the Resistance. 2,000 were executed while another 10,000 died in other ways during the War.

The stress and fear was everywhere. Everyone was on edge and the scared for themselves and their families. The specter of death was constant. In June, the Germans gave Jewish men married to Aryan Dutch women the option of either being sterilized or deported as they got rid of the Jewish mixed marriages. From May through September, the Germans conducted endless raids and confiscated the property left

Queen Wilhelmina spoke often on Dutch Oranje Radio, urging the Dutch to stay strong and to resist the Nazis. We all loved her (Photograph in Public Domain). A Dutch policeman looks out the hatch of a small bunker that served as a hiding place for Dutch Jews (holocaustresearchproject.org).

behind. Then the Germans would always ship anything of value to Germany. They were getting quite a pile of valuables in Germany. During this ramped up attack against the Jews, about 25,000 of them, including at least 4,500 children, went into hiding. About one-third of those in hiding were discovered, arrested, and deported. "Deported" doesn't seem so bad of a word, but it hid the truth of Jews being gassed by the thousands, shot by firing squads, starved, hung, beaten or worked to death. No one was safe and nothing was sacred.

The Germans were sending our people away by the trainloads. In September, the last of the Amsterdam Jews in the ghettos, who could be found, were sent off East. By the end of the year, over 150,000 Jewish men, women and children had been shipped away. Now, everything became more and more difficult for any remaining Jews.

Anne Frank and her whole family had hid in one place in Amsterdam, but normally that was not the case. Usually, the Dutch would go underground as individuals because of the dangers involved. Families couldn't afford to try to stay together because it was just too difficult and dangerous to find any place that would take in a whole family. With more people, it was easier to be found out. The more people, the larger the chance one of them would make a mistake. Over the next two years, I stayed undercover and on the run, living in a nightclub, camp, farm, home, church and camp again. I found out more about the Underground and the Resistance. All those university students who had been forced out of school had swelled the ranks of the Resistance. That group especially swelled when they were told by the Nazi party that they must sign an "oath of loyalty" to their German occupying forces. Most of them refused and thousands quickly went into hiding. It was the impetus of young people, quick minds and innovation that changed the Resistance and made it so effective. Soon these smart young people were illegally publishing their papers on an underground press and printing it in Polish, Yiddish and Hebrew as well as Dutch.

Much of the Dutch Resistance up until now was mostly passive resistance or non-violent active resistance, even with the strikes and a few assassinations. People would still listen to their illegal radios, often hidden in stairs, cupboards or attics. We were all hoping to find out what was really happening. Any of the radio broadcasts under Nazi control consisted principally of propaganda. The Germans had passed a law making it illegal to listen to British radio, but many of us quietly and carefully listened to the BBC and radio broadcasts from the Dutch government in exile. That, too, was stopped as the Germans confiscated over a million radios and fought any more resistance to the Nazis. Their acts of aggression inspired the Resistance to get stronger, more militant and braver. Weapons and explosives were sabotaged.

My way to resist was to live. Now, it was time I left my family and went underground. I regretfully left my family and headed out to hide from the Nazis. I left my "*Jood*" armband and took off all of the Stars of David on my clothes. I kept my false papers that didn't have the "J" next to my name. Mostly, I used my *koph* (wits) to avoid the traps set by the Germans. It was all about winning and my competitive nature wouldn't let me give up or get caught if there was a way I could avoid it. At 16, the risks were an adrenaline pumper. Life was always adrenaline followed by exhaustion and it wasn't long before I didn't even know how to handle a normal day.

When I had asked around about where I could hide out, a friend of mine told me I could hide out with him and his friends. Toskca, my friend, was a homosexual. Everyone loved him. By this time, Amsterdam had turned into a rogue city during the War with the Black Market, illegal nightclubs, sex parties and people with money trying to spend it before they died. As in all civilizations, there were class systems, too. There were, of course, the very rich, the middle class, and the blue collar group. I soon received an education in how some of the very rich spent their money. Toskca brought me to his home. It was

Germans setting up a gun at end of street and preparing to raid a street.
This is a poor quality picture but gives you an idea of what we saw
(Photographs in Public Domain).

my first hiding place and it was right there in Amsterdam.

Toskca ran an illegal nightclub with about four or five other homosexual men who were all actors by trade. But, at night they were running a popular underground nightclub. Now, this was early in 1943 and a large Black Market flourished. Some people were making fortunes by selling anything they got their hands on for enormous prices. Amsterdam was a wild city hidden from the Germans. Jews could hardly buy anything legally, so rich people looked for ways to spend their money. Others were more than willing to give them whatever they wanted for a certain price. The cabbies were horse and buggies because there were no cars. Those drivers would tell their customers about a nightclub and the drivers would get paid a small commission for recommending certain places. Wild living was an industry I had never known before.

The house itself was built in the 1800's. Sleeping was done in beds inside the walls with doors in front to keep warm – like a small room. The guys had converted one of those beds into a bar and I would be standing in there to serve drinks. Of course, they had 4 or 5 girls to entertain their customers. Things would become pretty wild sometimes with their sex parties.

Remember, the Jews had curfews and had to be off the streets at 8:00 PM and could not be out again until 6:00 AM. Our customers had to stay all night – once they were there, they had to stay until morning. Often I would find myself sleeping in a bed with a homosexual on one side and a beautiful girl on the other, with nothing sexual going on at all. As exciting as this life was, it worried me. Since our customers came because of word of mouth, more and more people knew about our illegal activities and that worried me. More and more people knew about the nightclub and the Gestapo was bound to raid it. So after a couple of months, I decided living there had become too dangerous, and I moved to the countryside. I left with a profound understanding and appreciation of my friends that gave me a place to stay, were homosexuals, their way of life and the life lessons I learned while I was hiding out with them.

Before the War, my family and I had camped in the province of Gelderland in the center of Holland. It was a beautiful tourist area. Being somewhat familiar with the area, I went back to the place that I used to go to camp in the summer time. I got a small job there cleaning and doing other things. There was something about being in the country, walking by the rows of ditches near the canals, breathing in fresh air and walking across green meadows that lifted my spirit. This was where I felt better and more hopeful. I worked there for the whole summer until the Germans started to come around. The people at the camp told me to be careful and when the Germans were around, I would quickly hide. Soon the Germans closed the campground and that ended that hiding spot for me and many others.

In the meanwhile, the people from the campground had put me in contact with a farmer who operated a large farm. I moved to this farm where I worked as a farmhand for some months. My job was to milk the cows and feed them. I took care of the horses, chickens and you name it, while they paid me with food and a safe place to sleep. My sleeping facility was in the hayloft of the barn which was directly connected to the house. I would sleep in the hay stack with some horse blankets. And, like a good farmer, I was wearing *klompen* (wooden shoes) to keep my feet dry.

While I was in hiding, I had no contact with my parents and was totally on my own. I was afraid to call them on a public phone in case it was tapped. That would put them in trouble and get me caught. I would sometimes sit there at night, when I could not sleep and bring out some of my many memories. In my mind, I would be back home with my family. I would think about the good times, before Leo had his breakdown, before

Mimeograph with bicycle used by Resistance to publish underground papers (Resistance Museum Amsterdam).
Resistance workers listening to their illegal radio
(Photograph in Public Domain).

Opa and Oma were taken and murdered and before the War even began. I treasured each of those memories and was thankful for their presence on those lonely, long nights.

What was a huge problem for everyone who was hiding out was the desperate need for food. Getting something to eat was the first thing you thought about, the main thing on your mind all day and the last thing on your mind when you tried to quiet the rumbling stomach at night. In hiding, I couldn't get coupons and without coupons, I couldn't buy food. With the job at the campground, I had been blessed to be paid with both room and board and a pittance of money. Before I had been able to barter for food, but soon the Germans tightened the "loop holes," making life more difficult in every way. They were everywhere on the hunt for a Jew to kill. Staying at the farm for now was the smartest thing I could do. They did not pay me, but they provided food and shelter that I needed. That was enough. I felt I was safe and I wasn't hungry all the time.

While I was working at the farm, I met a boy, Appie. He told me that his grandmother was renting a small room in the attic of her house. It was getting extremely cold and the barn was not at all comfortable any longer that winter. The farmer didn't

*Jews kept being rounded up and sent to their deaths
(holocaustresearchproject.org and Photograph in Public Domain).*

have as much work since there weren't any crops anymore and he really didn't need me anymore. So, I rented the attic with room and board. The attic was more like a very small loft at the top of a very narrow ladder. I could barely turn around and once I lay down, I pretty much just stayed put all night.

Now, I did not have to worry about food much here either. Appie's Oma was quite the lady. She grew her own vegetables and canned many of them. She had pigs, chickens and took care of everything. Her house had been built in the 1700's and was also connected to the barn. She told me how years before they would keep the cows in the house during hard winters. One day, this lady, who was in her 80s, picked up a sledge hammer and killed one of her pigs, hanging the 400 plus pound pig in her kitchen over the stove and dressing it out herself. She even canned some of that meat. It was delicious. For a Jewish kid from Amsterdam, this was one tough lady that impressed me.

Appie was a nice kid, but he was mildly retarded, or slow as we called it back then. We started a small business and he helped me. I needed to make money so that I could continue to rent the room. True, it wasn't too much, but it was enough to make me have to figure out how to sell something and make some money. The boy had a push cart and we would go into the woods and cut out dead trees and sell firewood by the load, paying the rent of about 25 guilders a month. And in the summer, we picked berries and sold them for one-and-a-half guilders a pound.

The name of the town where I was living was Nunspeet. It had been a tourist town before the War and it was a nice town, not filled with many Germans. The Germans here weren't so hateful of the Jews. Still, I tried to be very careful because you never knew who would turn you in. One day, we were selling berries at the house of the town's mayor and this kid, Appie, out of nowhere, said to him, "This friend of mine is a Jew." The mayor looks at me and started to laugh and said, "That boy sure can keep secrets, can't he!?" Thankfully, he didn't report me, but it reminded me that I had to be more careful. I asked the Oma if I could and she let me sleep between the floor boards for several days following that incident.

One large problem with living there with Appie's grandmother was that the next door building was a large hotel occupied by the German army. The soldiers would come to our house and ask me if I could get butter and cheese for them. It ended up that they would give me cigarettes and tobacco and I would trade with the farmers. They were just regular soldiers and family men drafted into the army. One of them one day said to me, "You are Jewish," and, of course, I could not say anything, but I could show him my falsified papers. He said to me not to worry at all about it because they did not care what I was.

During this time of hiding, I learned many important lessons about people, including who to trust and who not to trust. There were many nights I would think of my family and be frustrated because I couldn't be with them or even communicate with them. It was a difficult, hard War and I learned that even when people know better, they don't always do what is right. I also learned that fear can change a person who you think you know into someone you don't know at all. It was a very lonely time. I couldn't always trust someone just because they were Dutch and sometimes I was treated decently by a German. War was a confusing time for me, especially since I was so young and on my own.

When I look back to that time of hiding, I saw many things.

ABOVE: Letter similar to one I received, requiring I show up for work detail (annefrank.org/secretannex).
BELOW: Others who got the letter marched to concentration camp (Photograph in Public Domain).

Some things I saw and heard about I could not find pictures of, but they are there, burned into my memory. Many of the images still haunt me. Humanity cannot and must not forget what had happened in WWII. We must remember so that we make sure nothing like this ever happens again.

I distinctly remember the day a family was rounded up with many others. The Germans put them all in trucks to be transported to jail or to a concentration camp. A mother shoved her small daughter out of the truck and into the arms of a lady standing along the road. The mother yelled to the woman to take her daughter and save her. What a wrenching moment for the mother, the little girl and the person suddenly entrusted with this life. Moments like that would come suddenly and unexpectedly. These moments could easily switch between life or death, depending on split second decisions.

Being on the run and hiding, you hear these horrible stories. I was young, but wise enough to know that they were true. These stories haunted me then and still haunt me now.

I remember the story about the German soldier herding Jews into trucks and a little Dutch girl was crying. He grabbed her by her pigtails, swung her up and threw her into the truck on top of people already in the truck. Threw her like so much trash to be disposed of.

I remember hearing about the mother who had a very young child, just a baby, and they were trying to hide from the Gestapo, but the baby was crying and wouldn't be still. The mother put her hand over her own child's mouth and nose, stifling the crying, but in the end smothering to death her own child, trying to save its life and the rest of those hiding.

I still have pictures and images in my *koph* that fill my dreams and nightmares. There are certain smells and sounds that still disturb me greatly. Those of us who lived through the War are unable to outlive what we lived – it is forever a part of us.

Chapter Six: 1944

This was one of the hardest years for all Dutch people. The War went on and on, much longer and much harder than many of us had anticipated or even believed we could survive. This year was such a see-saw of emotions and physical difficulties that it was hard not to give up on the future. Some parts of our country were liberated during the year and other parts felt the crushing wrath of the Germans, trying to make sure they didn't lose control. Hope would wash over us, only to leave again and be so far away from us. Then came the winter and the wicked "revenge" of the Germans, which together, was almost a lethal blow to our people and country.

About the middle of January, I suddenly realized I had completely forgotten my 17th birthday in December. The Oma who I was renting a room from had a small "celebration" in December, mostly for her grandson, Appie. There was definitely no Sinterklaas. It was a quiet "celebration" and not much of anything to be celebrated except that we were still alive and free. The boy and I were still making some money or goods trades by going into the forests, finding wood and then selling it. Sometimes we saw German troops and we would lay flat in the grass or snow and watch them very carefully, if we could. Even from a distance, they struck fear in my heart for I knew that if they caught us, they would probably kill both of us or worse for me, send me to a work camp until I died. I was almost to the point that I didn't care about myself. I didn't want to die, but the hiding and scheming wore on me, and on everyone, and made me exhausted of the whole depressing situation deep within my core. I missed my family and I was so worried about them. They were always in the back of my mind and I hoped they were safe. I couldn't afford to think of them for too long or I would get too homesick and I had to keep my focus on surviving so I could see them sometime in the future. I was

143

Klompen – wooden shoes – often worn in Holland especially on farms (Photograph in Public Domain).
The barn I stayed in was similar to this one (canadaatwar.com).

LEFT: Removal of street signs with Jewish names in Amsterdam (holocaustresearchproject.org).

BELOW: Collage of signs against Jews (Photograph in Public Domain).

just 17 and wanted the chance to have a real life after the War.

My mother worked hard to keep Jews hidden and alive during the War. She risked her life every day. She did what these people had been doing for me that hid me. I always felt that in some way it was her way of helping me even though she could no longer personally help me. I was a draft-age young man and I was hiding out from the Nazis. I made it very risky and dangerous for anyone who helped me. I, and, many others, will always be deeply grateful to those who cared enough to go against the Nazis for us. We will always be grateful to the *onderduikers* (undergrounds) who saved so many of us Dutch desperately trying to stay alive when the enemy wanted us wiped out of existence.

More and more people from the cities came to our rural area looking for food, coal, wood to burn, even clothing. The War had dragged on for so long that many of the essentials were hard to come by. In the cities, people could buy small portions of food, coal and other basics, but only if they had coupons. If people were hiding from the Germans, as I was, they had no coupons and had no way to get them safely. The Black Market and bartering were thriving and we were a part of that as we sold the firewood and any coals we could dig up to anyone who had any money or something we could use. No matter what transaction took place, there was always the tinge of fear because this person could easily turn us in. Many had turned others in with devastating consequences. I really could never trust anyone and that in itself is debilitating. You could never let your guard down. That meant that there was never a real restful night or a time to relax. I was always on guard and had to be if I was to survive.

Finally, spring came and it wasn't as physically hard on the people, except for the constant need for food. It seemed we were stuck in this interminable chain of getting food, eating food and trying to get some more. We kept hearing of the Allies attempting to break into occupied Europe, but the Germans had fortified the coasts well. The Germans put up all kinds of posters showing the horrors of the Allied invasion, warning all Dutch people NOT to help the Allies and to run from them because of the death and destruction they were bringing to us. Most of us didn't believe their propaganda.

During this time, I was still living with the Oma and her grandson, Appie. The Germans were always upset by something and seemed looking for trouble, especially now that the Allies were getting closer. They showed their forces by deciding to round up most of the young men around Nunspeet. This was frightening to me and I was agitated and did not know what to do about the fact that young men were being picked up, so Appie and I went next door and told the German soldiers that if we would be picked up, they would have nobody to barter for them. They liked having us around because we would be sure to get them the things they wanted and they had a lot more stuff to barter with than anyone else around. They didn't want to lose our services so they gave us a couple of shovels and said to tell the soldiers who were doing the round up that we worked for them. We did and were safe. Some people complained and

Place in stairway where radio was hidden at home of watchmaker Corrie Ten Boom and her family from the book "The Hiding Place" (Corrie Ten Boom Museum).

when I explained my situation they understood. Appie relied heavily on me, which I did not mind because he was a very nice boy.

No, I did not get picked up in the Nunspeet sweep, but the War was about to become terrible for me. Back at Nunspeet, after they had taken all the men from the village, about three weeks later, I was downtown waiting to cross the road when two German police on bicycles were coming towards me and I knew I was in for trouble. Because I had escaped the round up, I had gotten less careful, but with all the men gone, I stood out like a sore thumb. Sure enough they stopped and asked me for my ID because they said they thought that I was Jewish, because of my nose, which I denied because of my false papers. They didn't care if I had papers or not; they would do what they wanted to do. I tried to tell them that I worked for the soldiers next to where I lived. They would not listen to me and arrested me.

They took me to their headquarters and they kept me there for a couple of weeks, cleaning their pistols and guns. Then, finally they put me in one of their trucks and took me to the Gestapo jail in Zwolle. This was a scary ride because by now the British planes were all over the place and we stopped several times because they were strafing the roads and were shooting at us.

Any successes of the Allies made the Germans even harsher with us, if that was possible. Upon arrival in Zwolle SS jail, I was thrown into the Jewish section of the jail where the tension was very high due to the fact that they had just executed some Jews in the prison yard. While in that jail, I got a sense of how awful it was for those who had been caught. While they thought of me as a Jew, the guards treated me like a dog, beating me easily and putting me in my place, kicking and hitting me. I endured a week of harsh interrogation because they thought I was either a Jew or spy and they made me suffer with continuous physical abuse. They fed us weak soup and dry bread. The cells stunk from feces, urine and wet, moldy straw. The last time they had been cleaned must have been before the War. The sense of hopelessness and fear was concentrated in these cells for Jews. The fear I had before I was in this jail was borne out even beyond my imaginations. Even though I was later moved out of the Jewish section of the jail, I saw cruelty, brutality and raw evil. There are times that it is very difficult to remember the specifics except that it was terribly cold.

After more than a week of cruelty, they brought me in front of the commander of the jail. He was an intimidating officer sitting behind a desk in his office with some other officers standing behind him. This did not bode well for me. He started out in the German language to tell me that I was a dirty Jew and called me some other names. I told him that he was wrong and that I was not a Jew. He was so enraged that drew his pistol and pointed it at me. He said that if I said I was not a Jewish again, he would shoot me. Brazen as I was I answered loudly, "I'm not a Jew!"

Then the next thing that happened was that one of the officers who stood behind him whispered something in his ear. After that the commander of the jail told one of the officers to get somebody. After about ten very long minutes, he came back with a German medical officer who looked at me and told me to drop my pants, which I did. He looked at me again and said to the commander, "He is not a Jew." Now, what had happened was what I talked about in the beginning of my story that my parents had a hotel, restaurant and bar in Ostende, Belgium, and my father had an accident and on account of that, when I was born, I did not have a traditional Jewish Bris, which is circumcision. I believe the commander of Zwolle would have shot me dead with his pistol if I had been circumcised. That lack of circumcision now saved my life and saved me from being sent to a concentration camp for the time being.

After that, they decided that I was not Jewish, but I was young and strong so they put me in their labor camp that was housed in an old school house with a dirt floor, smelly straw and not enough blankets. It had only one entrance/exit, so it was easy for the Germans to guard us. Every day, they would take us to various places to work on the German bunkers and this went on for some time, with no breaks and no letting up of the pressure. The Allies were getting closer and the Germans were frantic to stop them or face the wrath of their Fuehrer. They pushed us, demanding more and more work at a faster pace and didn't mind beating us to get their demands accomplished. Our work gang would fall exhausted on our straw mats every night, never warm and always very cold. It turned out that during this time I was about 70 miles from Amsterdam, but only about 45 miles from my father who was in Westerbork but I didn't even know that at the time.

What I found out later was that my father had been arrested in August standing in a bread line three houses down from where we lived. Somebody had called the police because it was after 5 o'clock and, as a Jew, he was not supposed to stay in line after 5 o'clock. The Jews were only allowed to shop between 2 and 5 o'clock and the reason for this was that by that time, most stores were sold out of food. My father knew better, but years of being put down and living in fear, he was frustrated and knew his family needed the bread and pushed the rules.

First they took him to the jail in Amsterdam on the Weteringschans where they also had taken Anne Frank and her family about a week earlier. While he was in this jail, some Underground Resistance forces killed a high ranking German officer and in retaliation, the German police selected a random 36 people out of this jail to go to alternative holding cells. My father was fortunate and was not selected. They took the 36 prisoners down the street to the Weteringschans Square and had the prisoners standing on a heap of garbage. Next, they stopped all the people who were walking around in the Square (one of those people was my future wife-to-be, Anna, who was 15-years-old at this time) and forced all the people, including her, to witness the executions of all 36 men. That was one of the most traumatic things she experienced in her life.

Later I found out all this and the following information, that Anne Frank and her family had been arrested the week before my father and were sent on to Westerbork a week before my father was sent there. When my father got to Westerbork, the deportations had wound down. It turned out that he stayed there for the rest of the War. Since the beginning of the War, the Germans had deported over 100,000 Jews from Holland, who were all shipped to Westerbork where they would stay for a week or so and from there, they were put on cattle cars and shipped to Auschwitz, Sobibor, Bergen Belsen and Mauthausen and their annihilation.

As had been done for so long in this fashion, 93 trainloads of Jews left Westerbork, with the last one leaving in September. On this last trainload leaving Westerbork, the Franks were shipped to Auschwitz. Because my father had come later than the Frank family from the Amsterdam jail, and because no more trains left Westerbork after that, my father stayed in Westerbork. On 12 April 1945, Canadians liberated him and hundreds of others. There were 876 prisoners, of whom 569 were Dutch. My father was forever grateful to the Canadians. Of the over 1,000 passengers on that last train out of Westerbork, over half, including children, went directly to the gas chambers, but that wasn't the end for Anne and her sister. Their end came within a month of liberation.

Then came 6 June. The Germans were taken by surprise with D-Day's success at Normandy, France. We even heard about it at Zwolle. The Allies had landed on European ground! D-Day happened in France, but the reverberations reached our country and every country occupied by the Germans. This was a turning point in the War and when the Battle of Normandy ended in August, much of the German resistance collapsed. The Allies were on their way to our borders, too. The Germans had caused such disaster and trauma on so many people in so many ways. For what?! Some cult that believed in some Aryan master race, its supremacy and destroyed wonderful, beautiful talented people who were "unfit" by their demented criteria?!! Some German Empire?!

During this summer, the Germans tried hard to completely finish up their destruction of the Jews, including the ghettos, all across occupied Europe. They wanted us all to be dead. By now, most Jews and other "unfit" people had been sent off to camps or killed. Our ghettos were pretty much empty except for some hidden away Jews who barely surviving and were shot if they were found. These empty buildings, walls and barbed wire fences of the ghettos no longer held life, but that had never been their goal. It was all about death. They were reminders of what had been ripped from Holland. It was eerie and dangerous to be anywhere near these skeletons of the last few years of this War.

With the Allied troops making inroads, our people had hopes, but nature came against us along with the Germans. Holland was hit with a severe drought and famine. The crops withered in the fields and the gardens dried up. Food, which was already at a premium, now became almost impossible to obtain. People were again suffering for lack of nutrition and this next winter would devastate, almost obliterate, Hollanders who struggled to find food and thousands died of starvation.

In the first few days of September, the first reports came that Allied forces were on their way to free us Hollanders. It was all over the illegal radio programs. People were happy and ready to welcome our liberators. People were all getting very excited because of D-Day and the huge victory the Allies had when they landed in Normandy. The Dutch knew the Allies were advancing deeper inside Europe's borders and many of us were getting excited.

Hollanders were so sure that their turn would be soon, that Tuesday, 5 September is known as *Dolle Dinsdag* (mad Tuesday) because the Dutch started celebrating in the streets. Dutch citizens were so sure that they were only days away from being liberated, that they were dancing in the streets. The Germans were confused as if the citizens knew something they didn't. For sure, the Dutch were "mad," because it was another eight, long, weary, deadly months before all were finally free. Up until this, the Germans had been somewhat subdued for a couple of months because, I think, they thought they would soon get run over by the Allies, too. Our early celebration woke them up and made the Nazis furious and determined to make our lives more hellish than before. They were further enraged and clamped down on us Dutch with a mighty death grip. Areas that had earlier been nodded at were now used to cause us as much trouble, pain, discomfort and despair as possible. It was an added bonus to them if those measures caused our deaths, too.

So, even now, Hollanders knew the Allies weren't getting as far as they wanted to reach and the population wasn't sure if it would be in time to free us before we were killed or starved to death. It was getting toward fall, which meant cold and no more vegetation. Many people ate the grasses or leaves, whatever few there were, but all that would be dying soon, too. There would be no more places to get food and people were already getting desperate. The Netherlands needed a miracle and we were counting on the Allies. Instead, as the Allies made inroads into the Low Countries of Belgium, Luxembourg and us, the Germans became more abusive as they feared loss of control. Their Fuehrer was outraged at what was happening in his Kingdom.

Once in awhile, the SS would catch Resistance fighters who were protecting Allied paratroopers or soldiers and would make them stand in the squares of the cities. Then, to remind all of us who was in control, they would execute them in front of everyone as a way to stop anybody else from helping the Allies or Jews or anyone. Citizens were so fed up with their wickedness, they were going a little crazy. Death had once been frightening, but so many of them had seen so much of it that it didn't have the same initial effect on them as once it did. We had become used to death. As the Germans promised us death, those words could not hold the fear they once had. The Allies were in our country and more and more of us helped the Allies in any way we could while resisting the Germans in any way we could. The Allied troops came with hope.

D-Day was a huge encouragement to all of the Dutch and many more people believed in the light at the end of this horrendous tunnel. The Resistance groups swelled as people's resentment of the occupying German troops led them to

Zwolle jail where I was beaten, where many Jews were murdered and where I was almost killed for being a Jew. It is now a luxury hotel. Life can be ironic (Photographs in Public Domain).

willingly help hide and protect downed Allied soldiers. Many had been working hard against the Nazis throughout the War. Now there seemed to be an end in sight. Some estimates put the number of Dutch citizens who were directly involved in the Underground at fifty to sixty thousand patriots and caring Dutchmen. Other Hollanders would offer some assistance to people, but not consistently. If these Resistance workers were betrayed or caught by the Nazis, they would often be shot. Many thousands of Resistance workers lost their lives during the War and we will remain grateful for their sacrifices for their country and people.

Some of the riskiest behaviors were hiding enemies of the Nazis, usually in their own homes, which was very difficult in cities. This was punishable by death. Despite the risks, many Dutch people helped the Jews and other "unfit" humans, although about one-third of the people who hid Jews did not survive the War. Many, many Dutch have been honored by Yad Vashem, the Holocaust Martyrs' and Heroes' Remembrance Authority in Israel, as "Righteous Gentiles."

True, the Allies were trying to get to us, but they had their own politics and egos getting in their commanders' way. British commander Montgomery first suggested Operation Comet which was to be launched on 2 September in Holland and would secure several bridges crossing the Rhine into the North German Plain. Poor weather and heavy German resistance scuttled that plan. So while Paris celebrated the American liberation, Holland was not celebrating. Our country was hoping that the Allies would get their game plan together and liberate us, too. We tried to remain hopeful so the fear and despair that was just at the edges of our lives didn't swallow us.

Finally, in early September, the Allies launched Operation Garden Market to advance the Allies from the Dutch-Belgian border across three main rivers in Holland; the Meuse, Waal and Rhine to get into the northern part of Holland and from there into Germany. They also wanted to take out the V-2 launch sites near the Hague because they were bombing London incessantly and Churchill requested them be destroyed. Because the drought had put many of us in dire circumstances, our hope was for immediate salvation and we prayed for their success. I prayed for their success so I would be free of my captivity and slavery.

Garden Market didn't produce the desired results, partly because it was the fall, times of incessantly heavy rains. So, the rains followed a drought where there was nothing alive to hold the dirt in place and everything was awash. Silt was deep everywhere and that was tough for any kind of travel. Holland was assigned many Canadians who weren't familiar with this kind of terrain. Some of the Americans and British were in the same predicament. Our Highway 69, later nicknamed "Hell's Highway," was one of the major routes, but because of dikes topped with bushes and trees, drainage ditches and too soft ground on either side of the roads and in the *polders* (swampy fields), thick mud and silt, it became a killing field for the Allies. Many, many vehicles were stuck there with no way around or through. It was hard on the Allied troops and, therefore, on all of us in Holland. Gratefully, it was also hard on the Germans.

For this operation to succeed, the Allies needed the bridges along Hell's Highway. This was a huge airborne operation and English, Canadian, American and Polish soldiers came into Belgium, Luxembourg and Holland on gliders or by parachutes.

After the War, we found out that a lot of bickering and one-upmanship at the Allied upper levels affected what happened in our country. Montgomery's great idea of skipping our country's liberation and going straight to Germany and making a mad dash to Berlin affected his tactical methods. His foolish handling of the Scheldt Estuary area, which was full of elite

German soldiers, meant he never got it sealed off. This area had over 65,000 German troops, along with over 200 guns and 700 trucks, all which came into Holland by barges, small boats and freighters. These Nazi troops caused way too much loss of life to our country and to the Allied troops trying to help us. I, for one, wasn't too keen on Montgomery after, that but I surely loved the British troops I went with into Germany later on.

When the Allies reached Arnhem in mid-September, there was a much stronger resistance than anticipated. Eisenhower and Montgomery had underestimated the ability of the Germans to keep this part of Holland. Although the fight was desperate, with Americans and British soldiers joining in, the Allies could not capture the bridge at Arnhem. The river was not crossed by the Allies by enough soldiers to make any kind of real headway here in the southeastern part of the country. The defeat was devastating to many of us Dutch who had high hopes of liberation, not defeat.

Hitler was furious at what was happening in Holland and told his armies to implement the scorched earth "policy." This was a campaign to destroy docks, harbors and any man-made helps for navigating the waterways. Even many of his own officers didn't agree with or go along with his rage, thankfully, but the fighting kept going. British and American troops continued to fight the Germans west of the Meuse. At Overloon, the only tank battle ever fought on our land took place as the Allies fought for the bridges of the Meuse. The heavy rains made fighting miserable and difficult. The British lost a lot of tanks in this battle because the Germans had 88 Flak anti-tank artillery guns that were so fast, that if you heard them coming, you'd better hit the ground or you were dead. Almost 2500 casualties made this one of the deadliest battles in Holland. Finally, in early December, the Allies defeated the Nazis between the Meuse and the Peel marshes which was packed full of bogs and canals. This victory was very hard on the Allied troops because of its huge price tag in men and equipment. We will always be grateful for those wonderful troops who fought on and fought through to save us. This was part of the reason I moved to Canada and then to the United States after the War – these people were very special to all of us in Holland!

There are permanent cemeteries and memorials all over the Netherlands honoring the many thousands of Allied troops

British burning Bergen-Belsen to stop the typhus (United States Holocaust Memorial Museum) and a picture that haunts me because it was taken right after Auschwitz was liberated (from private pictures of American Pvt. Benjamin Oblaczynski – permission given by Debbie Book).

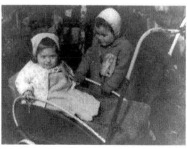

Jewish children waiting in line to be deported and killed. The Nazis murdered our future, too (Photograph in Public Domain).
Jewish child wears Jewish badge
(United States Holocaust Memorial Museum).

157

who gave their lives in battle for the Netherlands' liberation buried across our country. In the village of Margraten, six miles east of Maastricht, is the World War II Netherlands American Cemetery and Memorial war cemetery. Originally 18,000 American soldiers were buried there, but the now permanently remaining 8,301 dead Americans who died in "Operation Market Garden" fought in the fall and winter of 1944 are solemnly commemorated each year on Memorial Day (the Sunday in May before the United States' Memorial Day). In gratefulness, each one of the men buried in this cemetery and in the British and Canadian military cemeteries, has been "adopted" by a Dutch family. This family considers it an honor to take care of the grave and to decorate it as a way of keeping that soldier's memory in the forefront of the Dutch. Often this family keeps a portrait of their American, British or Canadian soldier in a place of honor in their home and often sends pictures of Memorial Day activities to that soldier's family.

Each Memorial Day ends with a concert. It is very moving and reminds us how much Holland will always show their gratefulness for those who made the ultimate sacrifice for our liberation.

Fall was over and the Netherlands entered one of the worst winters of our history. This winter of 1944-1945 was called the "Hunger Winter" (Hongerwinter) and was brutal on many of our people. There was neither electricity nor water in most of the northern provinces. Food was scarce or non-existent and people scrounged however they could for subsistence, often dying because they just could not find any food. The German occupiers showed true evilness as they made the winter much worse on all of our people. As the Allied troops liberated areas of Europe, the Nazis were angry and humiliated. There had been a famine in Holland at the end of the summer and into fall, but they would maximize the horrendous effects on our people by not allowing Allied food to reach us.

Our Dutch government-in-exile was desperate to help the people of the Netherlands. They gave orders for some Dutch railway workers to go on strike because they thought the Germans would soon be vanquished and they wanted to help the Allies. Unfortunately, there was not a German collapse, but instead the Germans gained their revenge against this strike by forbidding almost all food and fuel transportation to the west where over four-and-a-half million Dutch citizens were starving. People were fainting from hunger and most pets were cooked long before spring. This area, called the Randstad, is one of the most densely populated areas in the world and stayed cut off from food supplies into late spring of 1945 when Operation Manna was finally launched. Those long winter months took a huge toll on our people.

The winter came and was horrendous in this second half of 1944. People scavenged along silent and deserted railroad tracks for bits of coal, shops ran out of food and the Black Market prices soared above anyone's ability to pay. The ghettos and any houses vacated by Jews were stripped of wood and it was used as fuel. As the Allies tried to send supplies to our people, the Nazis not only refused to give them to us, but they all but stopped food deliveries to the northern Netherlands. Often they dumped those food stuffs to keep life from the dying. Thousands died with the end of this horrible War almost in sight.

City people were beyond hungry and would do anything to get food. They ate tulip bulbs, which smelled like chestnuts, or any type of bulbs, plants or vegetation. People were willing to walk for miles until they found a farm to trade with or to beg for food. Everything they owned was sold, (if they had anything to sell and if anyone had money to buy), to get something to eat. And for those that died, the ground was too hard to dig graves, so in Amsterdam the bodies were stacked in the Zuiderkerk

(South Church) and they would set up guards to keep away the rats. There was no wood for coffins.

A 13-year-old-boy was caught looting a store at night and was shot. His body was left in front of the store for days to warn others not to attempt stealing. The parks were bare as people scavenged the trees. People would cut the trees down, burn them in their stoves and stay warm for another day. This Hunger Winter lasted until spring. Over twenty thousand Dutch people starved to death, froze to death or just gave up and died. Severe malnutrition occurred and many women who were pregnant during that time often delivered unhealthy or underdeveloped affected children because of the starving mothers' lack of nutrients.

We all heard many stories, but one story I heard that made it real for me was about a teenager who came out of Amsterdam to the countryside to find food for his family. I met people like this every day at the Lutheran Church, searching for life in a land full of death. This particular young man walked miles and miles, searching for anyone who would help him and his family. The weather was brutal and he really wasn't dressed as warmly as was necessary, but he had no choice. Slowly, but surely, he collected potatoes and a couple of onions. Once he believed he had enough to feed his family, he began the long, arduous walk back to Amsterdam. The weather continued to beat him down and he was near exhaustion and almost hypothermic. He had to go through a German check point several miles outside of Amsterdam. The German soldiers stopped him and asked him what he was doing. He quietly explained that he had come in search of food for his family back in Amsterdam. The soldiers laughed and made fun of him, pushing him around. Then, the most aggressive soldier grabbed the lad's sack of potatoes and laughingly dumped all the potatoes into the canal. The teen watched in horror, slumped down into a heap along the fence

Cattle Car Memorial to the Deportees (Yad Vashem in Israel)
and inside of a boxcar
(United States Holocaust Memorial Museum).

Westerbork Jews called out and Westerbork "end of the rails"
(Photographs in Public Domain).

and died, soon covered with the blowing snow. That deep, relentless hopelessness pervaded much of Holland during this winter. We were all on the verge of giving up any remnant of hope just like that young man.

We were losing all of our young men. Our country was again stripped bare of any men who had not been arrested and taken in earlier raids. In November, in two days, the Germans rounded up 50,000 able-bodied men in and around Rotterdam and deported them to Germany. By now, people knew what was awaiting them and so did they, but maybe they wouldn't starve to death, although many did. No matter where we were, the hardships were unbearable and hope was a wisp of smoke in our dreams, for anyone who could still dream.

At this time, I was still working in forced labor of the Zwolle jail. I had seen way more than I wanted to see. Because they thought I was not a Jew, they had put me in the section with other Dutch young men working for them. Jewish men worked with us, but I saw the discrepancy. We were fed better than the Jews. The Jews were given smaller rations, less good food and easily beaten. As the Allies kept pushing closer to where we were, the guards got meaner and meaner, beating us all to push harder and do more. I could tell that I, too, was getting weaker. It wasn't good. When I look back, I don't remember a lot except that I was always cold and that horrible cold ruled all my thoughts.

When a person isn't eating properly, can't get warm and doesn't have the food necessary for the body to remain healthy, all parts of that body begin to fail. The mind often keeps us going beyond our body's ability, but it can't go on forever without nutrition. This failure of the mind was the beginning of the end for many Dutch people. There was no hope when the mind was starved.

Knowing our slim hold on hope, our guards enjoyed playing mind games on us. One of the worst nights we experienced

Dutch Resistance group in 1944 and with members of 101st Airborne Americans (Dutch Resistance Museum in Amsterdam).

was when the German guards told us on Christmas night that we would be transported the next day to Germany as forced laborers. Most of us were young boys away from home and the mood for that night was terrible because of what we knew would probably happen there, especially now with the Allies coming in and the Soviets coming from the East and neither knowing we were Dutch. I had just turned 18 and now feared that I would be sent to Germany to die for these tyrants. The next day, they told us that it was a joke, which we did not think was funny. They laughed and we slipped one more notch toward complete hopelessness.

Although there was not a lot of outside news that reached us prisoners directly, I got pretty good at understanding the Germans during this time. I would listen to whatever parts of their conversations that I could hear so that I would know what was going on in the War. At this time, they were feeling pretty good which caused all of us more despair because it meant the War was going badly for the Allies. It was the end of this year and there was the battle that later became known as the Battle of the Bulge in the forested Ardennes of Belgium, France and Luxembourg.

This surprise attack by the Germans turned out to be the costliest in casualties for the United States (89,000 wounded and 19,000 deaths) and lasted from 16 December 1944 until 25 January 1945. Germany wanted to split the Allies and recapture Antwerp and they almost succeeded because of Allied overconfidence in that the War was over and failure to read what little signs the Germans gave of this huge attack. The weather was overcast with a huge fog and grounded the Allied air forces for a time, but when the weather improved, the Germans were under attack and finally the offensive became a defeat for the Germans. But at the end of this year, it looked like the Germans would succeed and for all of us, it was a huge disappointment that the War did not end in success for the Allies by the end of this year. We felt deep despair and we would not truly escape it until the War ended in the middle of next year.

Chapter Seven: 1945, the Final Year

"The final year," behind 1945, I remembered when that year began and none of us was sure at all that this would be the final year of the War. The Battle of the Bulge was going badly for the Allies, thousands of people were starving and freezing to death and a lot of Holland was not anticipating liberation anytime

UPPER LEFT: German tank stuck along Hell's Highway (forum.nationstates.net).

UPPER RIGHT: Germans in the trenches near Arnhem (ww2incolor.com).

LOWER LEFT: American postcard about Hell's Highway (Photographs in Public Domain).

soon. I had been captured and was being worked miserably hard, with little good food. I was the German's slave to go out and work for them until I dropped dead or was shot by unknowing Allied troops. But, I was still alive and kept thinking about how to get home and find out how my parents, brother and his hidden wife and other family members and friends had fared during this War. Many Dutch people hoped our five year nightmare would end while we were still alive and some just didn't care anymore.

For the eight months I was in the Zwolle jail, I worked slave labor for the Nazis. The stress of everything I had gone through erupted in a serious outbreak of psoriasis. My skin was a big blob of red, itchy outbreaks. I was miserable. It was all over my body

LEFT: *Allied landings near Nijmegen, southeast of Amsterdam (Photograph in Public Domain).*
RIGHT: *The 506th 101st Airborne Division with Wild Bill of Band of Brothers drops near Grave (formerly De Graaf) (blackfive.net).*

LEFT: *British troops come in on gliders (Hartenstein Airborne Museum).*

except for my face and hands. So, I asked one of the guards if he could take me to the hospital for a checkup. He could see how miserable I was and called somebody from the medical office. I tried to explain to the doctor that what I had was hereditary from my mother's side of the family. But my explanation was in poor German so it turned out that what I said to him was, "Ich habben eine geschlechts krankheiten" What I said was that I had a sex-related disease. My poor German turned out to be a blessing because it frightened them.

That same evening, they told me I was released and to leave the building right away. Guess they didn't want whatever I had. Even our difficulties could sometimes be a blessing. I was put outside in the snow and quickly ran with only the clothes I was wearing. These were the same clothes I had been wearing for the last eight months. They had not been washed and neither had I. There were no showers or cleanliness for workers and I longed to go to the old Amsterdam bathhouse and clean up as I used to do so long ago. It was no wonder my skin erupted. I still can remember what I was wearing -- a pair of German booth riding pants, a riding jacket, a hat and a German poncho because they were the only clothes I had. Here I was, outside in the cold, dumped by the Germans, and trying to figure out what to do next. I kept carefully moving as I racked my brain as to where to go. I knew I couldn't go home to Amsterdam or back to the Oma's home with Appie. So, I decided to go back to the campground where I had started from, which was familiar to me and maybe afforded me a better place to hide and heal. If it was still closed, it would be the best place to hide. I could not handle being caught by the Germans again. I needed my *koph* to work and to work well.

One of my main problems was that I was on the wrong side of the river IJssel that connected one part of Holland with the other side. Nobody without a permit was allowed to cross the bridge. Not knowing what else to do, I started to walk toward that bridge, wondering how in the world I would get across. I did not relish trying to talk my way across with German guards who could grab me and put me back into that horrible slave labor. I shivered just thinking of that outcome.

When I was getting closer, a horse and wagon loaded with bags of potatoes was coming up to the bridge. I stopped the wagon and told the driver my problem and he said, "Get in the back and I will put some bags on top of you and take you across." This was a huge risk for this man because we both could have been shot if I was discovered. As we were starting to go over the bridge, the German guard stopped him, but he must have seen him before because he waved him on. I was lucky that it was raining. The soldier did not want to stay out in the rain, getting back into the guards' shack as quickly as possible. The driver of the wagon took me down about 25 more miles where he had to turn off for his farm. I thanked him profusely for his help and started to walk further in the snow and slush toward my destination. Finally, I reached a familiar place, the camp. It was very late at night and I didn't want to alarm anyone. I climbed through a window and fell asleep in one of the bunk beds.

The next morning, the people who had helped me before told me that I scared them when they first saw me in the bunk bed until they recognized me. As they gave me something to eat, they warned me that the German soldiers were all over the place because after the British attempt and landing at Arnhem last fall, they were constantly looking for British or any pilots. Also, by now the Allied bombers were going into Germany to bomb on a regular basis and planes would be shot down and many of the flyers would eject and land in Holland where the Underground would hide them and try to get them back to safety. It was more dangerous there than before and I had to leave.

Now, you might think that when they told me to leave that compound, my troubles would be over, but it was the opposite. I was right back trying to stay away from the Germans, still had my outbreak of psoriasis and still did not know where I could go to be safe. So, I had no choice again and had to leave. I thanked the people again for helping me. They told me about a Church in Ermelo that was known for helping people who were traveling from parts of Holland where there was a terrible shortage of food. People were dying from hunger. So that Lutheran Church became my next destination.

Now, I didn't just walk down the road like I was on an afternoon walk. No. I was just the age of young men that the Germans wanted and a young man like me, even with psoriasis, just walking along a road would soon be picked up and taken

Netherlands American Cemetery and Memorial near Maastricht (Photograph in Public Domain).

by the Germans. I was very careful and mostly kept to whatever woods or fields there were or traveled carefully at night. One thing I had learned very well was that there was still no safe place from the Germans and I didn't ever want to have them have their evil control over me again.

When I got to the Church in Ermelo, I was a little anxious. They weren't stupid; they knew I was hiding out from the Germans and was probably a Jew. But, they followed Jesus Christ and made the decision to take me in. It was a huge relief for me. They took me in and put me right to work, happy that a strapping young man would willingly work for them without pay, only some food and a place to sleep. They provided me with a small room with a bed in it, connected to the recreation hall. It was wonderful. I was safe again with a place with food and shelter and an opportunity to help my countrymen. It was a good place to be and I had a renewed zest to help out against the Germans.

A glimmer of hope broke through the dark clouds of War when about mid-March, Queen Wilhelmina came into the areas of south Netherlands which were occupied by the Allied forces through Belgium. Although it was supposed to be a secret, the Dutch people knew and passed the word along. They greeted their beloved Queen at every village she visited in the Walcheren region and in the city of Eindhoven where the local population went wild with delight to see her. Many of the Dutch wore their provincial costumes in honor of their Queen. She was kind to the many widows and reviewed the Dutch Marines, honoring them for when they stormed across the dikes to the Atlantic Wall, even though the Germans had boasted that no human power could breach the Wall. We all felt so much more hope now that our Queen was here. She loved her people and we loved her. Knowing what horrors her dear people had gone through, she refused to live in her palace when she came back after the War, and instead lived in a mansion in The Hague. She also wanted to be closer to the government and keep an eye on their behavior.

So, in parts of Holland there was encouragement and hope, but back at the Lutheran Church in Ermelo where I was living, we still saw much starvation and hopelessness. With all the refugees and people flocking here, there were meals to be made and sleeping arrangements for every evening. We were a refuge in the midst of the storm and it was my honor to make such a positive contribution to the people of my country. During the day, we would prepare for the evening by putting straw mats and blankets around the hall. People would come with everything that would move; bicycles, baby strollers, push carts and wheel barrows. They would bring anything of value to trade with the farmers for a bag of potatoes, some flour or anything of food.

In this fashion they would walk for miles to go to the farmers and then would have to walk all the way back to where they came from. One of the cities that was affected the worst was Amsterdam. Later, my mother told me that every day, from morning until night, the doorbell would ring and children would beg for something to eat. It broke her heart to see all these starving people and she couldn't even bring herself to answer the door anymore. By this time, too, there was neither electricity nor running water and no heat. Thousands and thousands of people were living on less than 365 calories a day. The most fragile Hollanders succumbed to the cold and starvation during this Hunger Winter. You know those little pats of butter you get in a restaurant to put on your bread? We would think that was a treat to be prized. After the War, my wife, Anna, would take any uneaten bread and butter from our table in a restaurant and bring it home. She never wasted anything after what we'd been through.

All day, I stirred those big pots of stew with potatoes and

whatever vegetables could be scavenged. I did it so that my people would live. We didn't often have meat, but it was always a treat if we could add any kind of meat to the stew. Rabbits were a delicacy and even they were running out. People would mill outside until they were allowed to enter the hall only at 5 PM and were received by me and someone else and we would direct them to a mat. After they were settled, we would serve them our hot stew that we had cooked during the day in those enormous pots. Every single one of them was very thankful for that and did not complain because it was a harsh winter and they walked in the rain and snow. Then, the next day, they

British Sherman tanks liberate Valkenswaard and British soldier on motorbike (Photographs in Public Domain).

Allied troops fighting from shell holes (histomil.com) and Canadians fighting (candaatwar.ca).

would leave and for us, it would repeat itself every day. We heard that the Red Cross was starting to hand out Swedish flour to some bakeries across our land and in April, planes dropped some food across the countryside, but it still wasn't enough.

One day, a young lady who was a neighbor of our family in Amsterdam came in looking for a meal and some shelter. She and her family were struggling, too. We talked and caught up with what had been happening since we had last seen each other. She told me my father had been arrested, but she didn't know anymore than that. Her brother had been shot for working with the Resistance. Although we both had been hurt, it warmed my heart just to see someone I knew and to talk about things I cared about because she knew my family. I found her a place and added a little more straw to her mat and gave her an extra ladle of stew. Since she and her friend were returning to Amsterdam with what food they had been able to gather, I finally was able to get a message to my mother where I was. That was a relief for me to connect with my family again, although now I was worried terribly about my father.

Before I came and lived in this Lutheran Church, the local Resistance had killed a German officer the previous fall near the small village of Nijkerk. In retaliation, the Germans surrounded the small town of Putten, which was a short distance from Ermelo. To the horror of everyone, the Germans then conducted one of the biggest Nazi raids ever done in Holland. On 1 and 2 October, they went from house to house, forcibly taking 661 men and boys and deported them to concentration camps such as Neuengamme and Birkenau. Only 49 of them ever returned after the War. Putten was known for many years as the town of widows.

One of the reasons I interject this story is to point out that, aside from the Jews, thousands of Dutch people died during the German occupation for many reasons. On account of that, we Jews cannot be selfish to think that we were the only ones to suffer. We must give respect to all the Dutch and others who died or suffered because of the Nazis, whose evil was an intolerable burden on our country and all of Europe.

More hope came to our suffering country when on 12 April, the Allied armies were involved in the Liberation of Arnhem, this time successfully. Many soldiers were in our area and it only took about three days for the Canadian Corps to take control of the city, which was now in ruins. The house-to-house fighting, which had become common in Arnhem, disrupted many people, but it was worth it for them to bring liberation. Also, the First Canadian Army was charged with clearing our country of all German forces. They were making headway, even if it was field by field. They had reached the banks of the Rhine

Troops in Battle of the Bulge
(Photograph in Public Domain).

*Troops in Battle of the Bulge and Christmas mass in a cave
(Photographs in Public Domain).*

in March and were continuing to root out pockets of Germans across Holland.

April was a month of hope, too, because we heard that Hitler had committed suicide. Many didn't believe it. We could not fathom that the maniacal mad man behind this Holocaust would not have had a backup plan, another means of escape or some other diabolical method of keeping the power he had worshipped. Many of us never did fall for the story that he and his mistress, Eva Braun, killed themselves. Whatever the truth was, enough people believed it and it was affecting his troops. We heard about more and more of his wicked minions being captured, being killed or committing suicide themselves. Many of Hitler's officers had disowned or abandoned Hitler before he supposedly died, hoping they could surrender and pretend their atrocity of a War had never happened. Well, it had happened and those of us to whom it happened were finally beginning to feel some sense of relief and hope.

The Allied troops were getting closer and closer to where I was in Ermelo. The Germans continued launching the V-2's at London. One of those launch sites was close by, based on a dairy farm. At night we would hear them going up into the air and we would listen for a special sound. If we did not hear that sound, we would dive into the cellar of the Church because those missiles had a nasty way to boomerang back at the launch site and explode. The bombs were built by prisoners who would sabotage them as their contribution to the Allies, but could end up killing the wrong people.

At this point, the Germans became very dangerous because many of them were deserting and would come through the village. People would sneer at them because, once a proud army, they now looked like beggars. Their uniforms were dirty and they themselves were an unshaven mess. German deserters were also stealing push carts and anything else they could grab to move their belongings on. The Dutch people hid everything and became very careful for what they did have to make sure these Germans did not get anything else from us. We were not so afraid of them now as we saw their strength dwindling and the Allied forces coming on strong.

Finally came the big day! Ermelo was liberated on 19 April by the British Armored Corps and by Canadians. Of course, everybody went crazy. The girls were kissing the soldiers who would give the men cigarettes and the children chocolate. This was, I assure you, beyond belief. After wandering for all those months, now I was able to walk around without looking behind me so much. But unbeknownst to me, as we were celebrating the next day, my father who was liberated from the concentration camp of Westerbork prior to us, was looking in the village for me. He had contacted my mother who had told him that I was hiding in Ermelo. The neighbor girl who was at the church had told my mother about me and where I was. My father never found me in Ermelo during that time and continued on to Amsterdam, afraid for what had happened to me. Afraid I was lost to him and my mother forever.

I had not known then that my father was looking for me. I did not know how his heart must have been hurting, wondering if I was still alive or if he would ever see me again. I did not know that he had gone back to Amsterdam with a heavy heart. I was focused on the wonder of liberation and freedom. I cannot explain the feeling, but I can tell you it was as if hidden away joy erupted in that village in such a way that people really did not know what to do with this long lost emotion. We all went more than a little crazy and it was alright because everyone was crazy with happiness and relief. There were many tears for different reasons, but there was much laughing and shouting, too.

Now I have to tell you something amusing to us in the midst of our celebration. In the center of the village of Ermelo, they had a traditional gazebo, where on holidays, a village band would play. And so this liberation was a good reason to have the

Bridge over the river Ijssel near Zwolle (Photograph in Public Domain).

band. The band was very enthusiastic and rather loud so that in the middle of our celebration party, there was a knocking from underneath the floor. Lo and behold, six German soldiers were hiding underneath the gazebo's floor! The noise was so loud that they would rather surrender than hear that noise any longer. They were taken as Prisoners of War by the British Army and we laughed about their surrender for many days.

As strange as it may seem, Canadian forces came into our country from Germany to liberate us. They crossed the Rhine at Wesel and Rees, freeing the eastern and some northern provinces. The western provinces, where the Hunger Winter was still devastating human life, had to wait until the Germans actually surrendered. A few days before the Allied victory, the Germans allowed emergency shipments of food, some Swedish Red Cross workers to bring some relief efforts and some air-dropped food parcels in Operation Manna. The Dutch would wave at the planes, crying with joy as they grabbed up the chocolate and crackers. It was something, but not enough in many situations. There were many stories of Dutch people dying just days or hours before the damnable Germans finally surrendered on 5 May in the Hotel de Wereld in Wageningen.

I have to tell you that during these horrific times, the acts of our liberators toward us civilians will always be a major point of endearment, friendship and even kinship between our countries. Although they had fought hard in this country on terrain that wore them out with mud and slogging through bogs, they treated civilians with such kindness. We loved them after the War and for many years afterward. These fighting men would share their rations, laugh with children, shake hands and hug adults, but mostly they encouraged us and treated us with respect and care, so much different than the Germans who hated us. As I told you earlier, it was because of their kindnesses to my people that I later immigrated to Canada and then moved on to the United States.

Forever etched in our history: 5 May 1945, Liberation Day, the day the Germans surrendered in Holland. The next few days and weeks were euphoric and chaotic. There was dancing in the streets and one man grabbed a Dutch flag and waved it back and forth, yelling, "I'm a Jew! I'm a Jew!" Everyone wore orange to symbolize the royal family. Girls wore bows and men wore armbands. People were taken out of hospitals to see the parades of Allied troops who had liberated Holland. Some people stayed inside because they couldn't handle all the celebration and shouting. They had gone through too much and their pain and agony was too deep.

There was also some lawlessness as Dutch citizens took revenge and the law into their own hands to settle some scores. Those who had collaborated with the Germans were abused and humiliated in public and sometimes killed. Their homes were looted and sometimes burned. Women who had relationships with German soldiers were despised, their heads were shaved and they were often painted orange so everyone would know that these Dutch women, called *moffenmeiden (Kraut whores),* had betrayed their country by being intimate with the *Krauts* (derogatory term for Germans).

All barbed wire fences were torn down, all signs against the Jews were ripped from their posts and fires burned anything left behind by the Nazis. Some businesses that had put up "No

Jews allowed" were burned. Holland wanted to be cleansed of the evil that had dominated our country and our lives for over five years. Tears, for many reasons, were shed across the land by almost everyone.

The particular division of the British Army that liberated Ermelo needed translators as they were moving into Germany. You know by now that I can be brash, so I told them that I was willing to go with them. They made arrangements for me and gave me a British uniform and I went into Germany with them. I remember well when I took a shower, with soap, and got to put on a new British uniform. I felt so different than I had only days earlier. Up until then, I had only one pair of underwear, had not taken a shower for months and wore the same clothing forever. Now, they gave me a couple of uniforms, several pairs of underwear and socks, but above all they trusted me and treated me well. I felt rich.

You probably cannot imagine how excited I was to be going along with the armored corps to Hamburg and after that, on to the small city of Bijenhouden where we were stationed in a castle. It was not that long ago I was stuffed into a jail in Zwolle. I had never seen a castle like that and it was interesting to see how the soldiers made themselves at home in those luxurious surroundings. I chuckled when early on I received a can of SPAM meat with eggs with my rations and I considered it a delicacy. Many of the soldiers around me complained about having to have SPAM again and some soldiers never would touch SPAM again after the War.

While we were staying at Bijenhouden, the British discovered a salt mine and took me down into the mines with some German guards. What they found in this mine was almost unbelievable. I could hardly believe what I saw. All against the walls were pictures and boxes full of valuable art that was taken from the Jews and hidden there by Goeble. It was not as rich as Merkers salt mines, but it was amazing. Salt mines afforded the correct temperature and humidity for the preservation of art. Within a year, Allied troops found art and treasure in over 1,000 repositories across Germany and Austria. There was much satisfaction knowing that Europe's valued art would be returned to the museums, collectors and galleries of our land.

As I spent time with these British soldiers, something happened to me. They treated me as a man, not as a hiding boy or as something despicable. They put me on an equal footing with them as a working man, appreciating my translation skills (even after I told them about my mess up with psoriasis being a sexually transmitted disease!) and appreciating my humor that I added to their lives. This was a turning point for me because I was wearing a uniform that stood for good and right. I was eating well and being treated well. Probably for the first time in many years, I wasn't afraid and I felt like a man should feel. It was a good place to be and changed how I viewed my future. It was an exciting place for me to be in Germany with the vanquishers.

While we were in this castle, the troops were thoroughly enjoying freedom from combat while lounging around in luxury. I wasn't the only one who was impressed by our castle. Many of the soldiers were like kids in a candy shop. Then, that escalated when a commander of this army group was approached by the Russians that they would like to give a party for us, which he accepted. A week later, three huge trucks came in to this castle loaded with food, drinks and you name it. But the real funny part was one truck was full of girls so that night they had a wild party.

The part that I liked was when the trucks stopped, the first Russian officer spied me and put his arms around me and kissed me on both cheeks and asked me my name. He spoke German so I said, "Cohen," and he started kissing me again because he was a Russian Jew from Moscow and he was glad to meet another Jew. It was a good experience to be valued because I was a Jew. I stayed with this outfit for about four months, translating for them. By that time, my English language was quite a bit improved except for the fact that this battalion was from London and spoke cockney English. So now, you had a Dutch Jewish kid from Amsterdam, Holland, who was speaking English with a cockney accent!

Things were winding down and the British were excited because they were shipping out to go back home. There was a lot of excitement and anything that wasn't nailed down was shipped back to England. I, too, was now ready to go home. In the meanwhile, I had acquired myself a motor bike. None of the British soldiers wanted one because they didn't want to figure out how to get it over the Channel. Regretfully, I said goodbye to all the friends I had made and went heading for Amsterdam, dressed in my British uniform! As I drove across Holland, many Dutch people waved at me on my trip and even gave me food and I even got a few kisses from beautiful Dutch women. Finally, because I knew exactly where to look, I saw Amsterdam and what a wave of emotions swept over me. I was going home. Home - the word caught in my throat.

Then, something I had dreamed of so many times actually happened. I arrived at the street my family lived on and, almost impossible to believe, I saw my father standing on the street, just outside the door to our house. Again, you cannot imagine how I felt to see my father, alive and in person, outside my home - as if he was waiting for me. I whistled a special whistle we used to call each other. Father looked around, but of course he did not expect a son of his in a British uniform. Then I called to him. This was a very emotional meeting. He was in terrible shape after his stay in Westerbork. He was badly beaten before the liberation of the camp and yet, he came searching for me in Ermelo! This son will always remember that huge act of love and sacrifice as he came looking for his lost son.

For the rest of his life, my father, like my brother, suffered from the problems of that War that had overwhelmed them. He lost his parents, two sisters, sister-in-law, nephew and niece, a brother and many friends. He lost his whole extended family to death in concentration camps. He thought he had lost me. When he talked about Westerbork, which wasn't often, he remembered walking past storerooms filled with women's hair and children's shoes. He told how, even in concentration camps, there were certain "positions" of power in the prisoners. He remembers prisoners fighting over a sliver of soap, people starving, beatings and sickness, with no medicine and no hope. My father was beaten badly and tortured while in Westerbork. He never quite completely came back to us. My mother, who was an absolute hero during all those years, took care of my father, my brother and Jetty. Jetty was glad to see me after that many long months. She, too, had a hard time of it and I will always consider her one of my heroes. My mother and Jetty were the definition of courage and determination.

I was so glad my father was alive, but like many Dutch, he was broken and traumatized, living in a ruined world. He was like the country, Holland, with its ruined economy, shattered infrastructure and several destroyed and ruined major cities. It would be a long haul out of this devastation, for the country and individuals, if it was possible. For years and years, both in the first and second generation, many received compensation from our government for they had been either physically and/or emotionally traumatized and were disabled. Many of Holland's people endured and continued to bear their crosses for all their lives.

Many, many people never recovered. One sacrifice that had started as an act of love, turned out to be disastrous for many families. Early on in the War, it was a hard time, especially for parents. Many couldn't bear the horror of losing their children to death, so Jews gave their children to Gentiles or sent them to other countries that would take them. England's Jews accepted children of Jews from many countries, including the Netherlands. Families were broken apart for the sake of survival and kind people took care of the children until the War was over.

Some Jewish families who had sent their children away to London or elsewhere or "gave" them to non-Jewish friends to keep safe during the War tried to reconnect with their children, but it was often traumatic, difficult or impossible. The children often didn't believe they were Jews or were still angry and hurt that their parents had sent them away. The parents and children could not bond again or the families who had kept the children wanted to adopt them, especially if the parents did not come back. But often the Jewish councils would instead give them away again to another Jewish family, which often caused more traumas for the children. Seldom did the reuniting have a storybook ending. Orphans had a particularly hard time of abandonment issues and some Gentile children resented their parents adopting other children. Many of those children grew up with issues that were never resolved positively.

We didn't even know about posttraumatic stress disorder back then. We just knew our people were in real deep trouble and no one had thought of how they could be helped. Churches didn't know what to do, the government did not have help set up for its citizenry who came back traumatized and families didn't know how to bond again. This was a very difficult time for every person in Holland, for the country itself and for our future. Many people never got the help they so desperately needed and therefore, never did recover.

There were two things that helped many of us put this atrocious War behind us in some way. First, as the Allied forces had discovered the horrific concentration camps and their despicable secrets, they did something all of us cheered. They forced the German citizenry, especially those near the concentration camps, those who smelled the putrid smoke billowing out of the crematoriums day after day – they made them help bury the bodies of the victims of the Third Reich. The Allied forces made the German men and women get out

However and with whatever they could, this is how people traveled (Photographs in Public Domain).

These pictures are very similar to what we saw at the Lutheran Church every day (Photograph in Public Domain). People searched along canals, railroad tracks and coal areas for coal or anything (Menno Huizinga in collection of Nederland fotomuseum).

*Arnhem children
with their
food parcels
(Photograph in
Public Domain).*

of their denial, locked behind their private doors. They made them get out into the concentration camps, to dig the holes, to move the dead bodies, to smell the rotting flesh and to give those people a decent burial and to face what they had allowed in their own backyards. The second thing that happened was when the Nüremberg trials began on 20 November 1945. The trials went on until 1 October 1946 when judgments for the political and military leaders of the Third Reich were handed down. Several of the defendants had committed suicide before the indictment was signed, including Adolf Hitler, Heinrich Himmler and Joseph Goebbels. The judgments handed down in 1946 against those who had collaborated with the Third Reich helped many of us find some closure. Arthur Seyss-Inquart was tried in Nüremberg, as were many other horrible, unspeakably evil men. The more deaths of them that we heard of, the better off was the world.

Our Queen was back riding her bicycle all over The Hague, visiting her people and refusing the amenities of her castle. The German soldiers were gone, many of the Nazi collaborators were identified and taken care of, and now we began the very long process of healing. When I look now at Holland and especially Amsterdam, I am not so sure the deep healing ever took place.

185

The following are permanent cemeteries and memorials in the Netherlands for the Allied troops who died in World War II, fighting to bring us liberation:

Australian, British and Canadian war graves:
- Arnhem Oosterbeek Airborne War Cemetery – 1,678 soldiers
- Bergen op Zoom War Cemetery – 1,200 soldiers
- Bergen op Zoom Canadian War Cemetery – 1,118 soldiers (of whom 971 are Canadian)
- Brunssum War Cemetery - 328
- Eindhoven (Woensel) General Cemetery - 700 soldiers
- Groesbeek Canadian War Cemetery – 2,610 soldiers (of whom 2.339 are Canadian)
- Holten Canadian War Cemetery – 1,393 soldiers (of whom 1.355 are Canadian)
- Mierlo War Cemetery - 665 soldiers (of whom one is Dutch)
- Milsbeek War Cemetery - 210 soldiers
- Mook War Cemetery - 322 soldiers
- Nederweert War Cemetery - 363 soldiers
- Nijmegen Jonkerbos War Cemetery – 1,629 soldiers
- Overloon War Cemetery - 279 soldiers
- Sint Oedenrode -
- Sittard War Cemetery - 239 soldiers
- Uden War Cemetery - 703 soldiers (of whom two are Polish)
- Valkenswaard War Cemetery - 220 soldiers
- Venray War Cemetery - 693 soldiers (of whom one is Polish)
- Werkendam War Cemetery - 23 soldiers (of whom one is Australian)

ABOVE: Moffenmeidens (Kraut whores) had their hair sheared for their betrayal with Germans (Photograph in Public Domain). Moffenmeiden tarred and feathered in Amsterdam (Nationaal Archief of Netherlands).

German soldiers surrendering to American soldiers, German POWs and another German surrenders (Photographs in Public Domain).

Member of the NSB and "moffenmeidens" led through the streets and were spat upon. Kraut whore sheared (Nationaal Archief of Netherlands).

Belgian war graves:

- Belgian Field of Honour 1940 (Maastricht) - 43 soldiers
- Belgian Military Field of Honour 1940 (Willemstad) - 153 soldiers
- Bergen op Zoom War Cemetery - 2 Belgian graves
- Dokkum Roman Catholic Cemetery - 1 Belgian grave
- Groesbeek Canadian War Cemetery - 3 Belgian graves
- Harlingen General Cemetery - 3 Belgian graves
- Holten Canadian War Cemetery - 1 Belgian grave
- Nijmegen Jonkerbos War Cemetery - 4 Belgian graves
- Vlissingen Noorder begraafplaats - 1 Belgian grave

French war graves:

- France Military Field of Honour (Kapelle) - 229 soldiers
- Beilen General Cemetery
- Schiermonnikoog Drenkelingenkerkhof Vredenhof
- Swartbroek (gem. Weert) Cemetery - 1 soldier
- Vlissingen Noorder Cemetery - 2 soldiers

Russian war graves:

- Russian Field of Honour Leusden (Leusden) - 865 soldiers

- Groesbeek Canadian War Cemetery (Groesbeek) - 1 soldier

Georgian war graves:
- Field of Honour of the Georgians under Loladse (Texel) - 476 soldiers

Polish war graves:
About 500 Polish war graves are located in the Netherlands.
- Polish Military Field of Honour (Breda) - 156 soldiers
- Polish Field of Honour Oosterhof (Oosterhout) - 30 soldiers
- Polish Field of Honour Ginneken (Breda) - 80 soldiers
- Polish Field of Honour Alphen (Alphen) - 18 soldiers
- Polish Field of Honour Axel - 22 soldiers
- Arnhem Oosterbeek Airborne War Cemetery - 73
- Schiermonnikoog Drenkelingenkerkhof Vredenhof - 3
- Werkendam War Cemetery - 1 soldier

U.S. war graves: All American war graves are located at the U.S.

Patton & Eisenhower inspect art in salt mines (Photograph in Public Domain). This is me in my British uniform. Too bad you couldn't hear my Dutch with the cockney accent.

Military Cemetery Margraten.

* U.S. Military Cemetery Margraten (Margraten) - 8,301 soldiers (originally 18,000 American soldiers in 1944/1945).

> *"Never was so much owed by so many to so few"*
> *- Prime Minister Winston Churchill.*

Chapter Eight - 1946 and On

The War was officially over and almost all troops had left most of Europe. But, the repercussions of this Great War lasted for years and years and years with hardship and shortages. My country also did not rebound for a long time. Neither did Europe immediately rebound. In my own home, I found I no longer fit in with what was left after the War. My father and brother were mentally, emotionally and, for father, physically debilitated from the ravages of the War. Our government paid us the normal stipend for disability, but nothing could bring back our beautiful life before Hitler's darkness ruined our lives. My wonderful mother kept steady and found a job and, God bless Jetty, she found a job, too. Every day was a difficult

British at Arnhem (Photograph in Public Domain). Canadian troops pass a windmill near Holten-Rijssen, April 1945 (militaryimages.net).

day at home and out trying to find work. I was finding that being home was almost more difficult than hiding out – it was stressful place to be.

Jobs were impossible to find, there was a huge housing shortage, food was still in short supply and everyone was still on edge. There was still rationing of cigarettes, material, laundry powder and coffee – even wooden shoes! Trust had been badly broken during the War and was still in short supply. Our government didn't seem to have the capability to handle all of this change and difficulty, along with the War in Indonesia against the nationalists demanding their independence. Queen Wilhelmina was frustrated with the politics and ineffectiveness of the government on so many fronts. She wearied of it and turned her monarchy over to her daughter, Juliana, in 1948. Most of us understood completely. In Holland right now, it was very hard to live, let alone thrive. I couldn't watch my family, day after day, the same, yet so terribly different.

Our Dutch government was angry and out for revenge and pay back. They tried to annex a sizable portion of Germany that would have doubled the land area of our country. The Allies refused, but they should have let it go through, especially since we later lost all of our colonies in Indonesia. After starting two World Wars, Germany should have been cut up into little pieces and handed out to Europe. The Netherlands still wasn't through with getting back at the Germans however we could and that included those despicable Dutch men and women, living on our soil, who had helped them.

Our Dutch minister of Justice Hans Kolfschoten, implemented a plan called Black Tulip to evict all Germans from the Netherlands. Lasting from 10 September 1946 through 1948, Germans with German passports were deported, kicked out. Over 3,600 Germans were deported by this method. Their homes and businesses were confiscated by the state.

They were grabbed in the middle of the night and given one hour to collect some luggage and could take only 100 guilders with them. They were taken to concentration camps near the German border, before being forced to leave the Netherlands.

ABOVE: Food handed out by 101st soldiers in southern Holland. Soldier treats our children well, being careful for their dolls (Photographs in Public Domain).
BELOW: American soldiers escort Dutch children to a concert celebrating liberation (Photograph in Public Domain).

They received the same treatment their people, our occupiers, had forced on us – only they weren't murdered. I have to admit that this seemed more than fair and it made us all feel a little better that we at least didn't have to compete against them for jobs and food in our own country.

There were some Dutch citizens who were known to have collaborated with the Germans and they were lynched or punished in various ways, not always lawfully. Some of our Dutch men who had fought with the Germans in the Wehrmacht or Waffen-SS were conscripted to clear minefields and suffered losses that seemed justifiable for their actions against our country. We were still reeling from the ravages of the Germans and we were not tolerant of anyone who had betrayed Holland.

Children waving at Allied planes and liberated Dutch waving orange flags – the traditional color of the Dutch monarchy and the beloved color for all the Netherlands (Photographs in Public Domain).

Germans surrendering to Americans (Photograph in Public Domain).

Actually, our War with the Germans had ended, but the Netherlands was now in another War that I would help fight. I was now 19 and had signed up for our military last year at 18. Let me tell you a little about the Dutch East Indies (Nederlands-Indië now called Indonesia). On 8 December 1941, the Netherlands government in exile joined the United States and declared War on Japan. The next month, the Japanese Military invaded the Dutch East Indies and never left until the end of the War. The real end of the War for them did not come until August 1945, when the Japanese Military were forced out of our colonies. When I first came home from Germany

LEFT: Flowers and smiles for our liberators
(Photograph in Public Domain). RIGHT: British tankers parade
through streets (wwii-netherlands-escape-lines.com)

Canadian tank going through Dutch street and citizens celebrating
liberation and freedom from the Nazis (Photographs in Public Domain).

last year, we were still at War with the Japanese Military and I signed up to go fight in Indonesia.

The Japanese Military despised Europeans and thought all of us as arrogant people. It seems that the Japanese Military had started talking with some Indonesian nationalists about taking their independence from Britain and us, the Netherlands. Once that can of worms got opened, those nationalists, led by a native named Sukarno, took over Sumatra and Java before the War was over in their country. When the Japanese surrendered on 15 August 1945, Indonesian nationalists declared their country's independence and fought a four-year War against the Netherlands. The colonies were a mess and now our country was asking for young men to go there and fight to keep our colonies from getting away from us. We couldn't afford to lose the oil-rich colonies.

I didn't leave Holland until January 1946. I first went to Britain where I was trained for about six months. I deployed to Indonesia and traveled on The SS New Amsterdam ship on its

Jewish child taken care of by a Dutch Gentile. Children saying goodbye to their parents (United States Holocaust Memorial Museum).

last troop voyage. When we reached Indonesia, I was thrilled to finally be someplace with lots of sunshine and really warm. The sun was hot, the ground was warm as was the water and I finally thawed out. Maybe it made me a little crazy. I was designated the bugler for our corps. Every morning I would wake our troops up with reveille to get everyone up and going first thing. Just to be a little crazy and add a little spice to the common bugle blowing, I streaked through the camp buck naked! The guys got such a kick out of my antics that they would follow me with the spotlight as I bugled my merry morning reveille around the camps. After that, they called me the naked bugle blower.

Fighting there was not all fun; it was very hard. We were following the Japanese Military who had killed 30,000 Dutch citizens and an untold amount of natives in Indonesia. The Indonesians often saw us as the same, but this was not at all true. The longer we stayed in Indonesia, the more we found out about the cruelty of the Japanese Military. There was much information we found out about the brutality of the Japanese Military that still haunts me today.

Before we were allowed to enter Indonesia, we were sidetracked to Malaysia to guard the Japanese POWs. The British Allied troops had captured Indonesia and they wouldn't let us in yet. In Malaysia, there was this huge runway and some buildings that we occupied. While I was there, we commented on the lack of young native men and women. There were plenty of older people and younger children, but hardly any young men and women. That's when we were told of the extreme cruelty and wicked deeds of the Japanese Military. Turns out the Japanese Military had used the young men to gather clay from about two miles away, bring it back to make the runway and then the young women had to stomp the clay to make it pliable and make the clay runway. If any of these workers fainted or were sick, the bulldozers would just run over them and they would be added to the runway. That's when we found out that runway was a mass grave with over 10,000 natives ground up into this Japanese Military atrocity! Just looking at that runway now and the beautiful scenery, no one would guess the horrors of its history. There were other horrible, unmentionable atrocities about the Japanese Military that I found out. Knowing all that horrible information changed our viewpoint of our Japanese prisoners and we were not so kind to them anymore.

For two-and-a-half years, I stayed and fought in Indonesia. The fighting was difficult because it was "guerrilla warfare" only we didn't call it that back then. We just knew that it was very hard and there were no fronts, just fighting everywhere. We were always on our guard because we did not know when the next attack would come and from where.

My job here was as an ordinance. I would take orders from headquarters to the different companies. I rode a motorbike on the roads as did anyone who carried orders. The motorbike had a hook welded to the front and this was because the Indonesians would string wire across the road, hoping to cut off our heads. It was a very dangerous time and we were always on edge so that sometimes we would need distraction. For entertainment, a few of us men would put on shows and such. I often played the guitar and it would relax us.

Nüremberg International Military Tribunal and the Palace of Justice
(United States Holocaust Memorial Museum).

After two years, we thought we were going to be sent home. All the preparations had been made. We had pretty much taken down camp and loaded most of our equipment on the boat. Then we got the orders that we would have a "shortee," which meant six more months of fighting. It was hard on some

German SS women are forced to bury Bergen-Belsen victims 28 April 1945. This was right after Margot and Anne Frank had died there (United States Holocaust Memorial Museum). Allied troops forced people from the town to view the mass graves (Photograph in Public Domain).

German civilians are forced to dig mass graves for the Dora-Mittelbau concentration camp victims. An American soldier makes sure they stay working at it (United States Holocaust Memorial Museum). German citizens from Nordhausen bury corpses of Nordhausen concentration camp prisoners (Joseph Mendelsohn collection - courtesy of United States Holocaust Memorial Museum).

ABOVE: Queen Wilhelmina and government returning to Holland, Queen bicycling around The Hague to visit with her people (Photographs in Public Domain).

of the troops because the hope of going home had been put out there like a carrot on a stick, then had been grabbed back. Troop morale was not very good for many weeks. Still, we fought hard and we finally left after those six months and went back to Holland.

Negotiations between the Dutch and Indonesians finally reached an end, leading to the Dutch recognition of the independence of Indonesia. Over 300,000 Dutch and Indonesians emigrated or returned to the Netherlands. You can still find their influence in our culture and cuisine. Speaking of influence, my father had taught me well during the War. He was in the Black Market and I watched and saw how he made money. In Indonesia, the way I made money was that I would buy liquor from the officers and sell it for a hefty profit to the Indonesian Chinese.

When Indonesia was granted its independence, it was time for me to go back to Amsterdam. I looked forward to seeing my family again, but I knew I couldn't stay with them for very long. I had changed. I had experienced a lot of adventure and still enjoyed life. My home was the same because my father's and brother's lives were basically over. It made me very sad to see them since I knew who they really were and what dreams they had – dreams that would never come true now.

I found a job, worked hard and married Anna Maria Hubertina, who was about four years younger than me and had been our neighbor. Still, there was way too much going on in my mind and life. I had a good job and worked in sales and design, but I just couldn't settle down in Holland. Holland didn't have room for me or many other Dutch citizens. About now, with the influx of people from Indonesia and the devastation from the North Sea flood of 1953 (where I took my sailboat and helped save many people but lost my sailboat in a terrible storm), the government encouraged emigration efforts to reduce our population.

The most popular spots to go were Canada, Australia and New Zealand. Anna and I migrated in 1954 to Regina, Saskatchewan, Canada. I worked for a furniture company for five years and we had two wonderful sons, Ted and Boyd. While there, I was a member of a Jewish society and directed the play, "The Diary of Anne Frank" for which I won an award in the Festival of Art. It was cathartic for me to direct that play.

We moved to Vancouver, Canada, but it was too wet and after two years, we got someone from the Barker Brothers Furniture Company in the United States to sponsor us to move to America. We had been in Canada for seven years. I was working for the Eaton Furniture Company and I really appreciated them. When my dear mother died, they sent a huge bouquet and gave me a week off. I will always appreciate that remembrance for my dear mother.

When we got to the United States, I was an interior decorator which was different than what they call them now for the Barker Brothers. After awhile I left to open my own company in

Los Angeles and Orange County. Royal Carpet and Drapes, my company, had seven franchises with over 100 people working for me. I separated from Anna and she took our boys with her.

In 1971, I met Jean Harriet Rosenblum, a beautiful Jewish girl from the Bronx. She was the secretary for my company in Buena Park and although our backgrounds were very different, our personalities were very compatible. We married in November, 1972, and worked well together since we first met. We started manufacturing statuary and we did that for five or six years. Then, together, we opened an importing company, J & J Design, which brought in ceramics, crystals from Austria and much more. We have traveled all over the world and seen many countries, enjoying meeting people the most.

My brother Leo died in the 1990's of lung cancer, but his wife Jetty, daughter, Lien Cohen and son Loekie Cohen, still live in the Netherlands (2014).

We retired in 2001 and moved to Murrieta, California, in 2002. We were retired for seven years and then couldn't stand staying at home anymore. We needed a challenge, so we opened up Old Town Boutique in Temecula in 2010 and have thoroughly enjoyed working here for the last several years. Stop by and visit!

This book is first published in 2014 when I, Jacques, am 87 years old and Jean is 80 years old and we've been married 42 years. We are great-grandparents, grandparents and parents of healthy and college-educated children, Ted, Boyd, Andrea, Robert (died in 2013) and Adam. We both believe in strong family and equality. We have a good family and a good life.

EPILOGUE

To bring an end to my story, I have to go back to the beginning.

"The Silent Cry" Memorial in Holocaust Museum in Jerusalem, Israel (Holocaust Museum in Jerusalem).

Forgive me if I've already stated these statistics, but on 10 May 1940, there were 140,000 Jews, including the 35,000 German Jews living in Holland. Of that number more than 107,000 Jews were deported mainly to the concentration camps of Auschwitz, Mauthausen, Sobibor and Bergen-Belsen. 5,000 outlived the horrors and came back. About 30,000 Jews tried to hide and of them, 15,000 were arrested by either being found out or by being betrayed. Over 75% of Holland's Jews perished. All in all, about 35,000 Jews survived the war, but a staggering 105,000 Jews did not survive and were murdered by the fanatics of the Third Reich. Maybe I'm repeating these numbers because I still can't get my head around what happened, what I witnessed and what I lived. Those numbers come out as just numbers and statistics, but they were living, breathing people who were fathers, mothers, sons, daughters with lives to live!

To whoever reads this story, I would like you to understand that I could not tell everything because many things happened in between and I did not write this story for anybody to feel sorry for what I experienced through those years. The main reason for writing this is that I would ask anyone who reads this and for anyone who sees the pictures that still don't communicate the reality of so much death to never forget what happened to 6 million Jewish people who died in the various concentration camps in Europe, plus all the other people in Holland, Europe and Indonesia who died by the brutality of Hitler's Nazis and the Japanese Military.

As for myself, I learned a valuable lesson at a very young age and that is to not have any prejudices towards any person or race, whomever you may be, black, white or yellow. Also, there must be equality for men and women and, most importantly, we must respect all religions in this world and by doing so, we might have peace in this world.

Throughout my life I have lived by those rules and hope the whole world would live that way so that the Holocaust will never be repeated. I now would like to finish with the words of Anne Frank, who wrote, "I still believe, in spite of everything, that people are really good at heart."

- Jacques Cohen

I share with you here the Cohen priestly blessing on you and yours. I remember when I still lived in Amsterdam, there was a small green door just a few doors down from where we lived where the Orthodox Jews would go to worship at the Synagogue. Women would go around and use a different door and would sit upstairs while the men would sit downstairs. The Torah and prayer rolls always stayed in the temple. I loved listening to the rhythmic chants of my Opa reading from these rolls.

"Cohen" means "high priest" (halakhically a priest) and Levie is the tribe from which the high priests were chosen. Cohen goes back to the Koathites who were given the task of packing up the Tabernacle in the wilderness. In that tradition, I, Samuel J. Cohen, now bless you, and if you fought for the Allies, I pray double blessings on you and yours, based on the scriptural verse, "They shall place My Name upon the children of Israel, and I Myself shall bless them." The blessing itself consists of the Biblical verses from Numbers 6:24-26:

May the LORD (YHWH) bless you and guard you -

יְבָרֶכְךָ, הוהי דְכְרְבְי

("Yebhārēkh-khā Adhōnāy weyishmerēkhā ...)

May the LORD make His face shed light upon you and be gracious unto you -

יְּנֶחִיוֹ, דְיֵלֶא וִיָנָפ הוהי רֵאָי

("Yā'ēr Adhōnāy pānāw ēlekhā wiḥunnékkā ...)

May the LORD lift up His face unto you and give you peace.

סוֹלָשׁ דְל סֶשׂיוֹ, דְיֵלֶא וִיָנָפ הוהי אָשׂי

("Yissā Adhōnāy pānāw ēlekhā wiyāsēm lekhā shālōm.")

Deep appreciation is offered to the war photographers who risked much to capture the images of this War. We, all people, are deeply grateful to your service and gifts to the world, showing us the reality through your pictures.

Sincere thanks must go to those who helped me and made it possible for my memoirs to be published: my dear wife, Jean, my encouraging children and friends who worked so hard on this book: Evelyn Nikkel, Irene Vogel, June Nagano, Zack Zeiler, and Glenn Van Wyhe.

Indonesian troops and fighters (Photographs in Public Domain).

Naked bugle blower is just behind the hut at the top of the ridge. (You did not think I would put in a close up!)

207

TOP: Queen Wilhelmina with a broken and restored tulip (TIME cover art in 1946 by Boris Chaliapin – found on flickr.com).
LOWER: Holland free at last – kicking out the Germans.
(Public Domain – Warandtactics.com).

209

S. Jacques and Jean Cohen

W e are contemporaries and survivors to unexpected events, accidents, experiences and an ever-unfolding history. When Hitler and his followers determined to purge the Jews, Samuel Jacques Cohen was a mere boy growing up in Amsterdam, Holland, unaware of any stigma associated to being a Jew. The personal life of S. Jacques Cohen has been correlated with many of the historical events of Holland during six long years from 1939 - 1946. In no time, the Nazi scourge and hatred would effect and change the course of S. Jacques Cohen's life, his family, Europe and the rest of the world. Jacques' coming-of-age-survival account during the Holocaust and World War II in Holland will offer unique insights into the most destructive, horrendous and life-changing events in the history of the world.

77981242R00122

Made in the USA
San Bernardino, CA
31 May 2018